MW01287331

"Juliet Mousseau
look at religious l
thoughtful and scholarly treatment is accessible and readable.
From a grounding in our Catholic tradition, Mousseau looks
forward to re-imagine the vows for twenty-first-century religious.
For those new to vowed life, it shows where we come from. For
those with a lifetime of experience, it shows where we're going."

—Amy Hereford, CSJ, Attorney/Canonist

"Juliet Mousseau's *Prophetic Witnesses to Joy* is clearly the most
up-to-date theology of religious life available. It is an integrated,
positive, theological, and experientially grounded exploration
of consecrated life within the context of the universal call to
holiness. A valuable read for anyone who desires to be a faithful
disciple of Christ and a must read for those involved in the
ministry of religious formation. A wise, refreshing, deeply human
witness to a joyful way of life from the new generation of those
who have found meaning in the life of vowed religious but
also valuable for anyone who desires to reflect once again on a
decision they may have made long ago."

—Donald Goergen, OP

"Grounded both in both historical tradition and contemporary
reality, Juliet Mousseau provides a much-needed, updated
theology of the vows for the twenty-first century. Mousseau
invites the reader to understand the vows as a way to follow
Jesus, make meaning of our rapidly changing world, and live
joyfully for the sake of the Gospel. Her book should be required
reading for elected leaders, formators, those in formation, and all
who believe in the present and future of religious life."

—Susan Francois, CSJP, Assistant Congregation Leader,
Sisters of St. Joseph of Peace

Prophetic Witnesses to Joy

A Theology of the Vowed Life

Juliet Mousseau, RSCJ

LITURGICAL PRESS

Collegeville, Minnesota

www.litpress.org

© 2021 by Juliet Mousseau, RSCJ
Published by Liturgical Press, Collegeville, Minnesota. All rights reserved. No part of this book may be used or reproduced in any manner whatsoever, except brief quotations in reviews, without written permission of Liturgical Press, Saint John's Abbey, PO Box 7500, Collegeville, MN 56321-7500. Printed in the United States of America.

1   2   3   4   5   6   7   8   9

Library of Congress Cataloging-in-Publication Data

Names: Mousseau, Juliet, author.
Title: Prophetic witnesses to joy : a theology of the vowed life / Juliet Mousseau, RSCJ.
Description: Collegeville, Minnesota : Liturgical Press, [2021] | Includes bibliographical references. | Summary: "An examination of how living a life of consecration calls into question the value of power, sexuality, and material possessions"— Provided by publisher.
Identifiers: LCCN 2021025158 (print) | LCCN 2021025159 (ebook) | ISBN 9780814666838 (paperback) | ISBN 9780814666845 (epub) | ISBN 9780814666845 (pdf)
Subjects: LCSH: Monastic and religious life of women. | Consecration of nuns. | Vows.
Classification: LCC BX4210 .M75 2021 (print) | LCC BX4210 (ebook) | DDC 255/.9—dc23
LC record available at https://lccn.loc.gov/2021025158
LC ebook record available at https://lccn.loc.gov/2021025159

I dedicate this book to the sisters who have gone before me
in gratitude for their witness
for their joy
and for their fidelity to Love

Contents

Preface

This book arose from a need I discovered while teaching a course at Aquinas Institute of Theology on the Vowed Life as well as my own personal drive to understand the life I chose as a Religious of the Sacred Heart. My formation in the congregation emphasized my need to place vowed religious life within the theological reality of the Christian faith. This book feels like a simple beginning to a process that takes more than a lifetime. I hope someone finds it helpful and that all who pick it up find in it the joy of witnessing the love of God.

Special gratitude goes to the religious women and men who have guided me throughout the years, especially my mentors and formators. From you I learned what real joy is, the joy of being known and loved by God. A profound thank you.

Introduction

At the core of our Catholic faith is the belief that God created everything that is, including humanity as a whole and each individual person in all his or her uniqueness. God is good, God's creation is good, and God put us here on earth to be as happy and fulfilled as possible in this life and completely in the next. To that end, God sent Jesus, the only Son of God, to save us from all the ways we turn away from God and to show us the way to God's kingdom. Since the death and resurrection of Jesus, Christians around the world have been seeking to follow Jesus faithfully, to find joy, and to make the world a better place. For some Christians, that effort leads to religious life, in which each one offers all that he or she is and has in order to dedicate everything to God and to seek out God's kingdom. This call to religious life is often felt as an irresistible pull, something that draws the person inexplicably to a lifestyle that is impossible to explain to others. It's obvious to many religious that God *wants* them and that though free to turn away, consecrated life is the path to fulfillment.

I truly believe that God wants us to live wholly fulfilled lives and that in our fulfillment we will find joy. What brings us fulfillment? Nothing other than following where God leads us. The prophet Jeremiah teaches that God has a vision of each one of us before we are born: "Before I formed you in the womb, I knew you; before you were born I dedicated you, a prophet to the nations I appointed you" (Jer 1:5). God knows what we will do, how we will live, and what will make us happy. It is in prayerful discernment and choosing

1

to follow that vision that we begin to live out the joy God imagined for us. The irresistible pull that I felt to religious life must have something to do with that dream God had for me. How on earth is that possible? What might that mean? How do I work that out for myself and for my life as a religious?

As a professor in a theological school, with students who are in religious life and others who are deeply invested in and working toward the kingdom of God outside of religious life, I strive to connect faith and life for myself and my students. Religious life is a bright light for our church and for our world, and yet many people have no knowledge or experience of this light. So, we keep trying to put it on the light stand once again, for all to see.

The historical and theological traditions of the Catholic faith provide support for religious life, beginning with examples from the first years of the church following the life and death of Jesus—and even before and during the life of Jesus, our Jewish ancestors had similar patterns of a life devoted to God. Other traditions in the world also include small groups of people who seek out more deliberate ways of living their faith. There is no way that this book can explore all these areas, and no reason to in light of all the resources available to us today. Additionally, many works exist to guide us in spiritual reflection on these topics—and so this is not a need that this book seeks to fill.[1] Instead, based on my background as a historical theologian, I will seek to draw in the traditions (history) of the church as I explore the theological

---

1. See bibliography for references on religious life. The most comprehensive is Sandra Schneiders's three-volume opus, *Finding the Treasure: Locating Catholic Religious Life in a New Ecclesial and Cultural Context* (New York: Paulist, 2000), *Selling All: Commitment, Consecrated Celibacy, and Community in Catholic Religious Life* (New York: Paulist, 2001), and *Buying the Field: Religious Life in Mission to the World* (New York: Paulist, 2013). Many of the resources listed in the bibliography also include reflection questions.

underpinnings of religious life today. The world around us changes constantly, and those changes must be considered in our exploration of theology. So, the question I seek to explore here is, How do we live out our call to religious life in today's world, as reflected in today's theological language?

In considering this topic, questions emerged. Exploring the call of religious life, particularly in the writings of Pope Francis, led me to language about following God in joy and hope.[2] Yet, it is clear in the tradition that these are not characteristics unique to consecrated persons. All Christians are called to follow Jesus, and all are called to see the joy and hope our faith brings and to share it with others. So, what is unique in this regard about religious life? Another theme that emerged with Francis and other theologians is the idea that religious are to be prophetic witnesses in our world. Much has been written about religious as prophetic witnesses to the gospel message, which brings hope and joy to the world.[3] Again, all Christians are called to witness to the Gospel, so where does the unique vocation of consecrated religious lie?

The answer seems to revolve around all these ideas. Consecrated religious hold nothing in reserve in order to live as prophetic witnesses of the joy and hope of the Christian message. Free from other commitments that take time and energy away from this role, they offer a radical commitment

---

2. See, for instance, Antonio Spadaro, " 'Wake Up the World!' Conversation with Pope Francis about the Religious Life," trans. Donald Maldari, *La Civiltà Cattolica* I.3–17 (2014).

3. See, for example, Michael Crosby, *Can Religious Life Be Prophetic?* (New York: Crossroad, 2004); Albert Nolan, "Religious Life as a Prophetic Witness," *Grace & Truth* 31, no. 2 (August 2014), 6–16; Mary Pellegrino, "Life on the Margins: Charismatic Principles for Modern Religious," *America Magazine*, October 16, 2013; and Donald Senior, "Living in the Meantime: Biblical Foundations for Religious Life," in *Living in the Meantime: Concerning the Transformation of Religious Life*, ed. Paul J. Philibert (Mahwah, NJ: Paulist, 1994), 55–71.

to God. Consecrated religious, then, are called to be prophetic witnesses, bringing the joy and hope of the gospel with them in the world, wherever they go and in whatever they do. The radical nature of their witness, its single-mindedness, points to the possibility of a new world, one that more closely resembles the world God imagined at the moment of creation. The unique nature of this call is the depth to which it is lived out in vowed life.

The new world that Christians hope for, God's dream for creation, is both here and now and in the future beyond time—in the here and now, it is a world in which human dignity is never violated, and in a future time and place it is a world in which human beings are united to their Creator. A life of consecration prefigures God's world, God's desire for creation, by calling into question the this-worldly values of power, sexuality, and material possessions. Consecration to the evangelical counsels challenges the importance of these things to human dignity. It shows that we can be more fulfilled, happier, more whole without attachment to them. And it shows that detaching ourselves from these desires allows others to live with more dignity and greater ease as well. Consecrated life, then, is a prophetic witness to the joy of the eschatological call of Christianity. In the words of Pope Francis to religious men and women leading up to the Year of Consecrated Life, "Wake up the world! Be witnesses of a different way of doing things, of acting, of living! It is possible to live differently in this world. We are speaking of an eschatological outlook, of the values of the Kingdom incarnated here, on this earth. It is a question of leaving everything to follow the Lord."[4]

By starting with the theological foundations for a life consecrated to the evangelical counsels, we can examine the prophetic nature of each vow, along with its model of the kingdom of God on earth and the reign of God in heaven. In each of these areas, imagining the possibilities of a better

4. Spadaro, "Wake Up the World."

world here and now and in the age to come bring hope for the future and radiant joy. Thus, religious men and women are called to be prophetic witnesses to the joy God wants all of us to share.

It might be that the theological understandings professed here seem to be the same as what others have been writing about for centuries, and of course that is true. Our faith is an enduring reality; it is not something that changes. Yet, the Christian faith has only endured for two thousand years because the expression of the faith has been adapted to suit the world's changing needs. I hope the expression of the faith presented here is particularly suited to the world as it is today, increasingly non-Christian or anti-Christian, politically and religiously polarized, with greater connection among nations and at the same time increasing fear of those who are different. While the creed we profess forms a stable foundation of belief, the world changes at a remarkably increasing speed. Our faith must be able to speak to those changes, or it will lose its timelessness.

In this rapidly changing context, religious life, too, finds itself shifting. While there has always been an ebb and flow of membership in religious congregations and movements, the remarkable decrease in numbers over the course of a single lifetime since the Second Vatican Council seems shocking to those who lived through it.[5] A closer glance at history can help put this change in perspective, yet understanding it does not diminish the need to respond.[6] Women and men still long for spiritual meaning and purpose, and many still seek out the

---

5. These numbers are so frequently requested that the Center for Applied Research in the Apostolate (CARA) has a chart at the top of its webpage. See https://cara.georgetown.edu/caraservices/rellife.html. For more demographical information on the changes in religious life, see Mary Johnson, Patricia Wittberg, and Mary L. Gautier, *New Generations of Catholic Sisters: The Challenge of Diversity* (New York: Oxford University, 2014).

6. Diarmuid O'Murchu, *Religious Life in the 21ˢᵗ Century: The Prospect of Refounding* (Maryknoll, NY: Orbis Books, 2016). Pages 64–67 discuss

vowed life as an expression of their life's longing.[7] Religious life and expressions of religious charisms find themselves in need of constantly renewed engagement with the world as it is today. Our life and charism are enduring, but they will become irrelevant if we isolate our language from the changes going on around us. In any relationship, when one side finds itself in new circumstances, the other side must adapt to the relationship or lose the connection altogether. Religious life that is not woven into the fabric of the world has lost its mission, given to us by Jesus Christ himself. New movements in theological language must be applied to the theology of religious life today in order to actively engage in the needs of the world.

This tension between the rootedness of the Christian tradition and the whirlwind of passing time forms the context of the prophetic witness religious life offers. Prophecy marks the grief and hope of our present moment in light of the identity we know from our past and the vision of newness for the future.[8] As Walter Brueggemann so clearly articulates, the prophetic witness of Christians offers critique of the contemporary status quo while imagining the newness of a hopeful future. Oppression and injustice, and all other forms of death, must be recognized and mourned. Then, the desire for newness, for change and a better life for everyone, awakens. The longing for change opens the way to the prophetic imagination of a future that more closely resembles the ideal world God saw at its creation.

---

one approach to a cyclical history of religious life, one that bears out this change in demographics across 2,000 years.

7. CARA's regular studies of religious men and women are helpful guides to trends among those entering religious life. See https://cara.georgetown.edu/caraservices/rellife.html.

8. These two elements of prophetic witness come from Walter Brueggemann, *The Prophetic Imagination* (Minneapolis: Fortress, 2001).

While all Christians are called to be prophetic witnesses, the religious man's or woman's interior and exterior freedom and deliberate focus on relationship with God place emphasis on this call in a special way. As the Congregation for Institutes of Consecrated Life and Societies of Apostolic Life (CICLSAL) states, "The time of grace that we are living through, with Pope Francis's insistence on placing the Gospel and what is essentially Christian at the centre of things, is for consecrated men and women a new call to watchfulness, to be ready for the signs of God."[9] The freedom of detachment as articulated in the evangelical counsels allows our eyes to be completely open for the signs God reveals to us. Religious occupy a unique space in the church—neither clerical nor lay,[10] on the inside but also on the margins; in the world, and yet critical of it by vow. Religious women and men witness to the joy of a prophetic vision for the world, a joy which comes from deep faith and trust that the powers of the world do not and will never overcome the power of the Creator God. This joy is not unfounded—and the strength of this joy comes from knowing and deeply experiencing the grief of death in all its forms that plagues the world. Mourning opens the way for new life that can be imagined once the old ways are judged insufficient. Mourning makes way for imagination, enthusiasm, hope and joy, to let go of the ways of oppression and open the door to God's Beloved Community.[11] As consecrated religious, "We have to fight against eyes weighed down with sleep, so as not

9. CICLSAL, "Keep Watch! To Consecrated Men and Women Journeying in the Footsteps of God" (Vatican City: Libreria Editrice Vaticana, 2014), 7.

10. Though, technically speaking, religious life is integrated into both clerical and lay lifestyles, in practice and common sentiment it lies between the two realities.

11. Historical roots of the phrase "Beloved Community," popularized by Martin Luther King Jr., can be found here: https://thekingcenter.org/about-tkc/the-king-philosophy/.

to lose the attitude of discerning the movements of the cloud that guides our journey and to recognize in the small and frail signs the presence of the Lord of life and hope."[12]

This book will present a theological basis for the prophetic nature of consecrated life. Chapter 1 focuses on theological anthropology, the *imago Dei* instilled in each human person that offers meaning and dignity. Our *imago Dei* means that we share in God's essential characteristics, first among them being freedom. In freedom, we discern our path, surrounded by others who form a community modeled on the Trinity of persons that is God. It is from this human foundation that women and men choose to consecrate their lives in the evangelical counsels of obedience, poverty, and chastity.

The second chapter continues the foundational elements of religious life by examining the integrated whole of living by the three vows. While the three vows are treated separately in the following chapters, here they are examined as a coherent life form that evolves from the time of the prophets to the present day. Through commitment, the religious finds a depth of freedom that is not possible without commitment. This life commitment will be shown as a prophetic witness to the hope and joy offered by the Christian faith.

Chapters 3, 4, and 5 examine each of the evangelical counsels separately. Beginning with obedience, they are demonstrated to be a witness to the path lived by Jesus for the church today. Each one is a prophetic challenge to the status quo of the world as it is now, offering a countercultural witness to a world that is different and renewed. This prophetic witness in each vow points to a future world here on earth and existence beyond the grave in the promise of resurrection to eternal life with God. Hope for a better world is the foundation of our joy as Christians and a witness to others that our faith is real and alive.

12. CICLSAL, "Keep Watch," 7.

One final impetus for writing this book comes from my experience of religious life among religious of many different congregations. Since my very first days as a candidate in my community, I have participated in the national group Giving Voice, which draws together women religious under age fifty for conversation, companionship, and shared leadership.[13] In Giving Voice, I found my companions on this journey, women who entered religious congregations singly or in groups of two. Our shared experience of formation, community, and generation allowed us to grow in friendship. While my call drew me to the Society of the Sacred Heart, and I find myself at home in my congregation's charism, the call to religious life in general gave me a second home among women from many congregations in Giving Voice. My hope is that this book speaks in some way to all of us. As Pope Francis and others have articulated in the last few years, there is a common charism (or "global charism") of religious life shared by all women and men who have committed to it.[14] My experience in Giving Voice showed me that long before I heard anyone else speak of it. Knowing that all our differences represent unique facets of God's reign only gives brilliance and color to the kingdom of God. May we find in one another motivation to follow the individual calls God offers each one.

---

13. See www.giving-voice.org.

14. Márian Ambrosio, "Weaving Solidarity for Life: Living and Witnessing as Women Religious of Apostolic Life" (keynote address presented at the International Union of Superiors General Plenary Assembly, Rome, May 9–13, 2016), http://www.internationalunionsuperiorsgeneral.org /wp-content/uploads/2016/04/Pl-2016_Marian-Ambrosio_ENG.pdf; Mary Therese Perez, "Local and Global: Charism of Religious Life Today," in *In Our Own Words: Religious Life in a Changing World*, ed. Juliet Mousseau and Sarah Kohles (Collegeville, MN: Liturgical Press, 2018), 67–81.

CHAPTER ONE

Foundations of a Call

Introduction

Jesus calls his followers to holiness, urging repentance and declaring that God's kingdom is coming. At the same time, his actions show us what it means to strive for the kingdom in the present time. Thus, the message is about right now and at the same time about the future world. Ultimately, he is calling us to our fulfillment, to eternal happiness with God in heaven. As children who grew up in the first half of the twentieth century learned from the *Baltimore Catechism*, "God made me to know him, to love him, and to serve him in this world, and to be happy with him for ever in Heaven."[1] Deciding how to work toward that fulfillment requires a call to conversion followed by a lifetime of discernment. The initial discernment results in a life direction that varies widely from person to person. One focus of the Second Vatican Council was to eliminate the hierarchy of holiness among human persons. The document *Lumen Gentium* (LG; Dogmatic Constitution on the Church) in chapter V, "The Call to Holiness," asserted, "all in the Church, whether they belong to the hierarchy or are cared for by it, are called to holiness, according to the

---

1. *The Baltimore Catechism*, lesson 1, q 6.

apostle's saying: 'For this is the will of God, your sanctifica-tion.' "[2] Thus, every Christian person is called to follow Jesus. Whereas the *Baltimore Catechism* taught that holiness was best lived as a priest, second best as a sister or nun, and only third best as a married man or woman, the Second Vatican Council declined to place one way of life over another. "It is therefore quite clear that all Christians in any state or walk of life are called to the fullness of Christian life and to the perfection of love, and by this holiness a more human man-ner of life is fostered also in earthly society" (LG 40). Since the council, which marked such a dramatic shift in thought, theologians have further expressed the value of single life as a way toward holiness. Married life, parenthood, single life, consecrated celibacy, ordained priesthood—all are paths that lead the committed Christian toward joy and God.

Holiness, then, has been democratized. "The forms and tasks of life are many, but holiness is one—that sanctity which is cultivated by all who act under God's Spirit and, obeying the Father's voice and adoring God the Father in spirit and in truth, follow Christ, poor, humble, and cross-bearing, that they may deserve to be partakers in his glory. Each one, how-ever, according to his own gifts and duties must steadfastly advance along the way of a living faith, which arouses hope and works through love" (LG 41). Each way of life allows for growth in holiness and greater union with God. That said, each one is different and by its nature involves distinct commitments that guide the path of holiness. Christians are all called by Jesus to act with faith and compassion, bringing his message to others. With these universal calls of Christians in mind, how do those who have consecrated their lives to God live differently? How does this particular path to God

---

2. *Lumen Gentium* 39. Quotations of Vatican II documents are taken from Austin Flannery, ed., *Vatican Council II: The Conciliar and Postcon-ciliar Documents* (Collegeville, MN: Liturgical Press, 2014).

bear witness to Jesus in a unique way? How does it offer happiness to those who live it?

Church documents have attempted to answer these questions by presenting the prophetic nature of consecrated life, in which the living out the evangelical counsels becomes a sign of the holiness to which all Christians are called:

> The growing awareness of the universality of the call to holiness on the part of all Christians, far from making the belonging to a state of life particularly adapted to the realization of evangelical perfection superfluous can become an added motive for joy for consecrated persons. They are now closer to the other members of the People of God with whom they share a common path in the following of Christ, in a more authentic communion, in mutual respect, without being superior or inferior. At the same time this awareness challenges them to understand the sign value of consecrated life in relation to the holiness of all the members of the Church.[3]

As a sign of the holiness of the church, consecrated religious can find joy in pointing the direction to the way of Jesus in ordinary life.

This initial chapter on theological anthropology places religious life in the context of what it means to be human—the reality shared by everyone on earth, as understood in the Christian context. Theological anthropology gives meaning to basic assumptions about our lives: why we were created, where sin and evil come from, how we are in relationship with God, what it means to be a human community, and how we find fulfillment in this life and the next.

---

3. CICLSAL, "Starting Afresh from Christ: A Renewed Commitment to Consecrated Life in the Third Millennium," (Vatican City: Libreria Editrice Vaticana, 2002), 13, https://www.vatican.va/roman_curia/congregations /ccscrlife/documents/rc_con_ccscrlife_doc_20020614_ripartire-da-cristo _en.html.

Theological Anthropology:
A Starting Point for Meaning in Life

As human beings, we ask big questions, and these questions help us to formulate and understand our faith. How did the universe come into being? Who am I? Who is God? Why do bad things happen to good people? What am I longing for? Perhaps the most fundamental of these questions is "Who am I?" The Christian tradition finds an initial answer to the question in the book of Genesis, where God creates human beings. In Genesis alone there are multiple explanations of how humans, along with everything that exists, came into being. Each of these stories tells us an important part of the truth of our existence.

In the beginning of Genesis, God is a transcendent, all-powerful Creator (Gen 1:1–2:3). God creates the universe, the earth, and its creatures, culminating with the highest of the creatures, the human being. God creates human beings on the sixth day, declares this creation to be "very good," and then rests on the seventh day. God makes human beings male and female, all in the "image of God" (Gen 1:27), and God gives them responsibility for the created things that came before them. By creating humanity in God's image, God gives human beings some of God's very own characteristics: goodness, reason, creativity, responsibility over the created world, generativity, and especially freedom. God also implants within them a longing for God, some sort of heart-knowledge that they are incomplete in this world. As St. Augustine famously put it, "Our hearts are restless until they rest in you, O God."[4] Thus, from the beginning, human beings have sought something greater, something that fulfills the longing deep within. "The believer seeks the living and true God, the Beginning and the End of all things, the God not made in his or her

4. Augustine, *Confessions*, trans. R. S. Pine-Coffin (London: Penguin, 1961), 1.1.

image and likeness but the God who made us in his image and likeness, the God who makes known his will, who indicated the ways to reach him: 'You will show me the path of life, fullness of joys in your presence, delights at your right hand forever' (Ps 16:11)."[5]

In the second account of creation given in Genesis (2:4-25), God becomes a master artisan, who shapes human beings from clay and then breathes life into them.[6] Here, human beings are artistically designed. Later Scripture speaks of the artistic care with which God shapes each individual human person: "How precious to me are your designs, O God" (Ps 139:17). Humans are made from the very earth itself. In this version of the creation story, men and women are shaped separately, the man first (Gen 2:7, 20-24). God then takes a rib from the first man and fashions the first woman around it, stating that he needs a companion. Without giving details, God creates man and woman separately, and so affirms that there is something distinct about them. By creating a companion for the first human person, God affirms that human beings are not meant to be alone.

After relating the goodness of creation, Genesis turns to the first hint of evil. Though God stated that human beings are "very good," God also gave them freedom, and freedom opens the possibility of making bad decisions. The first sin is hubris: Adam and Eve disobey God in the hope that they can gain some knowledge that does not belong to them (Gen 3). As much as human beings are good, they are also open to and even inclined to choose the wrong and to hurt themselves and one another. Any act of sin turns one's face away from

---

5. CICLSAL, "*Faciem tuam, Domine, requiram*: The Service of Authority and Obedience" (Vatican City: Libreria Editrice Vaticana, 2008), 4, http://www.vatican.va/roman_curia/congregations/ccscrlife/documents/rc_con_ccscrlife_doc_20080511_autorita-obbedienza_en.html.

6. Translations differ as to whether human beings were shaped of "clay" (according to NAB) or "dust" (according to NABRE).

God and God's love. Of course, this is not what God had in mind when God endowed the human person with freedom. God's dream for us does not include us turning away. Yet the freedom to act in goodness must also allow for the possibility of acting badly. Thus, in making human beings in the *imago Dei*—the image of God—God endowed them with the freedom to choose the good, and with that freedom human beings brought evil into existence.

God's desire for humanity is that they use freedom as God does: to choose what is good and loving. When we follow the path God laid out for us from the moment of our creation, we are progressing toward the fulfillment of God's great dream for us. Because human beings are as diverse as the breadth of God's imagination, each one's path is unique. For most, fulfillment comes from marriage and family life; for many, following God's law is less conventional. For some, God's path leads to consecrated life. A life governed by the vows of poverty, chastity, and obedience seeks always to move closer to God. Like all other human beings, those following the path of consecrated life sometimes stray from God's vision for them, seeking fulfillment in other directions. Yet, when consecrated religious discern carefully and stay on that path, they strive to follow Jesus toward the Father. This imperfect striving to fulfill the vows of poverty, chastity, and obedience is the way consecrated religious become more *human*, so that we also become more divine. "This is the primary mission of the consecrated person: he or she must witness to the freedom of the children of God, a freedom modelled on that of Christ who was free to serve God and the brothers and sisters, and moreover to affirm with his or her very own being that that God who formed the human creature from clay and knitted that creature in his or her mother's womb, can form his or her life, modelling it on that of Christ, the new and perfectly free man."[7]

7. CICLSAL, *Faciem tuam*, 15.

The Genesis accounts of the creation of human beings demonstrate that humans are "very good," that they are created to be in relationship with one another, and that freedom is central to their identity, part of the *imago Dei* they were endowed with. The creation stories reveal an intimate relationship between the Creator and creation, most especially with human beings at the center of the created world. God created each human person to reflect a bit of God's own self, expressed as freedom, responsibility for creation, creativity, and love, among other characteristics. This act of creation also reveals the intimacy of a relationship between human beings and God. God did not have to create anything, and yet God's love overflowed in creating the abundance of human life, meeting all our needs with generosity. While God would have remained God without creation, God's love needed expression. Creation—including the creation of human beings—was an act of love. It marks the beginning of a relationship between Creator and created that rests in this love.

The whole Bible tells the story of the relationship between God and humanity, which is marked first by the covenants of the Old Testament. "The covenants between God and the people are all covenants of divine favor or grace. They express God's gracious commitment and faithfulness and thus establish a continuing relationship."[8] By covenant, God promises to protect and provide for the people, to be "their God." The people promise their fidelity to God. With this, the Israelites become God's people, the chosen ones whom God leads to the Promised Land through the mediation of the prophets.

The love story between God and human beings finds its height in the incarnation. The self-gift, self-emptying of God to become human in the person of Jesus Christ, is the center

---

8. Bernhard W. Anderson, "Covenant," in *The Oxford Companion to the Bible*, ed. Bruce M. Metzger and Michael D. Coogan (New York: Oxford University Press, 1993), 139.

of the Christian story. As a way to repair the sinfulness that humans fell into and to save us from eternal death, Jesus takes on human form and dies for our sins though he had no sin. "No one has greater love than this, to lay down one's life for one's friends" (John 15:13). This gift of self into poverty, lived in obedience to the Father as a gift of love to the people, will be explored at length in a later chapter. Jesus's life and death add to the story of human creation by emphasizing the holiness of the human person, made in the image and likeness of God. By becoming human, Jesus Christ showed us how we are called to live and gave a concrete human example to follow in our own lives. With the creation and the incarnation as guidance, we can begin to understand three significant foundations of religious life: discernment in freedom, the call to mission, and the support of community life. Permeating these three elements of religious life, prayer and contemplation support the call to consecration and life on Jesus's path.

Discernment in Freedom

Freedom is constitutive of the human person. It is one element of the *imago Dei* that defines the human ability to make decisions and to act out of them. Freedom as understood by theologians differs from the common societal or political conception. While many understand freedom as the license to choose whatever one wishes to do, freedom in the theological sense is particularly directed toward what is good, toward life in holiness following God. Thus, freedom is lived rightly when it is in pursuit of a holy life. Pope Francis, in *Gaudete et Exsultate*, states it like this: "Do not be afraid of holiness. It will take away none of your energy, vitality or joy. On the contrary, you will become what the Father had in mind when he created you and you will be faithful to your deepest self. To depend on God sets us free from every form of enslavement and leads us to recognize our great dignity."[9] God created us for this holy freedom. Freedom is malformed when it results in taking actions that are contrary to God's will. Thus, while allowing for evil, freedom is true when it leads one to choose what is good. Freedom exists on multiple levels, only one of which refers to external limitations. On this external level, one's freedom is expressed in relationship with other people and with the material world. Freedom in this sense might be limited by commitments made and honored, by external moral or legal codes, or even by physical limitations or access to goods or power.

Internal freedom exists on the mental and spiritual levels. This freedom is expressed through the capacity to make choices based on faith and out of love for others, with spiritual and emotional flexibility. Internally, freedom can be limited by attachments to material things or people or places, by mental blockages or illnesses, or by negative thoughts or impressions. This freedom demands discernment, which is an attitude and practice of listening for God's movement and voice within. Discernment helps human beings to obtain interior freedom and choose what God is calling them to. It involves listening to internal and external factors in such a way that one hears the voice of God leading one to a particular path. Regardless of which path a person follows, "the important thing is that each believer discern his or her own path, that they bring out the very best of themselves, the most personal gifts that God has placed in their hearts" (*Gaudete et Exsultate* 11). Discernment will be addressed further in chapter 3; here, we will focus on examples of discernment in freedom from the Christian tradition.

9. Francis, *Gaudete et Exsultate: Apostolic Exhortation on the Call to Holiness in Today's World* (Vatican City: Libreria Editrice Vaticana, 2018), 32, https://www.vatican.va/content/francesco/en/apost_exhortations /documents/papa-francesco_esortazione-ap_20180319_gaudete-et-exsul- tate.html.

Discernment among Jesus's Apostles

Called to follow in the footsteps of Jesus, Christians must listen to God's call in order to discover what that path looks like for them. "At its core, holiness is experiencing, in union with Christ, the mystery of his life" (*Gaudete et Exsultate* 20). The first to do so were the apostles. The call narratives from the gospels are a little abrupt. Jesus, walking along, comes upon people doing whatever they do in their ordinary lives, says to them "follow me" or "come and see," and they immediately drop what they are doing to follow him. Such charisma! What is it about the call of Jesus that makes following him irresistible?

One answer might be that the men Jesus calls were searching for meaning, and Jesus offers purpose and a message that they can integrate into their lives. The man Jesus preaches the message and also lives it in word and action. The gospels illustrate his care for the dignity of each human person. He heals the sick and comforts those who mourn or are bound to the guilt of their sinfulness. He teaches people that love and care for others should guide our choices. He feeds the hungry and gives drink to the thirsty. His message is consistent, challenging, and countercultural. He consistently favors the ones who are rejected by the powerful. He challenges the status quo, treating people from all walks of life with dignity (e.g., the woman accused of adultery in John 7:53–8:11, and tax collectors and sinners in Matthew 9:10-11 and Luke 15:1-2). He challenges those who consider themselves holy to see the holiness in the unexpected places (as he does with the Pharisee who watches the tax collector pray in Luke 18:9-14). His actions and miracles work toward healing, feeding the hungry, removing demons, and assuring safety. Jesus's message is that God's plan includes a better life for everyone, a time and place in which all are well, no one goes hungry, and all humans have dignity. The Beloved Community Jesus preaches is both on this earth and in another realm. The apostles witness to the actions and words of Jesus, following him in order to understand better and ultimately being sent out to pass on the message of the kingdom of God and the need for repentance.

The Twelve are by no means the only recipients of the call to follow Jesus. Tradition holds a special place for Mary Magdalene as central to the announcement of Jesus's resurrection. In the history of the Catholic tradition, she was called "the apostle of the apostles," reflecting that after her arrival at the tomb early in the morning, she announced to the Twelve that Jesus had risen from the dead. In the midst of such sorrow and discouragement, she brings light and hope. Like the apostles, Mary Magdalene hears Jesus call her to follow him, and she stays with him throughout his ministry, even being with him at the foot of the cross.

The interaction between Mary and Jesus at the tomb (John 20:11-18) reflects the deep knowledge that God has of each one of us, from before we are born. Jesus speaks Mary's name, and she knows to the depths of her being that he recognizes and loves her. He knows everything about her, and in hearing his voice she sees her friend Jesus through the image of the gardener. The power of that interaction points to our deepest human desire to be known and loved by God. In that utterance of her name, Mary's long-standing search for completion is fulfilled in God. Mary is seen in that moment—for all that she is, for all that she feels. In the midst of deep darkness, she feels the astonishing love of being known by Jesus. Known and loved, she is called to act, to witness to the apostles the truth of Jesus's resurrection.

Following Jesus led Mary Magdalene to the foot of the cross, where she experienced the anguish of losing a beloved friend in an act of violent injustice. Opening one's heart to being known and loved by another likewise opens the heart to the heartache and grief of loss. Mary's inability to see the resurrected Jesus in the garden shows her anguish following Jesus's death. She is blind until he speaks her name—identifies her, calls her by her deepest self. The complicated emotions of these unexpected events are unimaginable two thousand years later. As Mary's anguish becomes unimaginable joy, her astonishment sends her out to proclaim the good news of the resurrection to others who are still held by sorrow and fear. Amid Mary Magdalene's sorrow, she remains on the path Jesus laid out for her, accompanying him to Calvary and his body to the tomb. Even in her loss, she is openhearted, able to hear God's call to her. Grief over the injustice turns to amazement at the fulfillment of the promise.

The call to religious life depends on recognizing ourselves in God's voice calling us. Like Mary Magdalene, we hear the voice of the one who loves us and recognize our fulfillment in the love offered.[10] Jesus knows us to the very depth of who we are, and he loves us without reserve. The power of that love is all-embracing, humbling, perhaps a little intimidating, and it empowers us to go out and love others as well.

Much like Mary Magdalene's path, discernment, whether to religious life or another life-form, leads to a fulfillment that does not promise constant optimism or an absence of grief. Discernment can lead directly to the pain of loss. It is not about feeling good or pleasure, for feelings do not lead to lasting fulfillment. Instead, listening in discernment helps us to see meaning, to secure a life of purpose that extends beyond our individual lives. That purpose comes to align with God's will through ongoing, constant listening in prayer and contemplation, so that we can say with Christ, "My food is to do the will of the one who sent me and to finish his work" (John 4:34).

---

10. A spiritual exploration of this is found in *The Sacred Gaze: Contemplation and the Healing of the Self* by Susan R. Pitchford (Collegeville, MN: Liturgical Press, 2014).

Discernment in Christian life, and especially in consecrated life, forms the foundation of action and witness. Walter Brueggemann speaks to the call of every Christian to radicality on behalf of God's message to us. This prophetic witness begins with critique, calling into question the elements of death in the sociopolitical world around us. Following critique, the prophet must energize the community in hope for newness, for a world that leads to life rather than death.[11]

Mary Magdalene's actions as she follows Jesus provide a demonstration of this call to prophetic imagination. Her friendship with Jesus gives her a foundation of self-knowledge and relationship that allows her to see the reality of the world with clarity. As she accompanies him to the cross and the tomb, her grief reveals the depth of destruction found in the world. Death is present, unjustly dealt to her beloved Jesus. Weeping and unable to recognize him, Mary knows the inhumanity of the world. Yet, hope lies in her too, hope stoked as he reveals the truth of the promise: that he has conquered death and offers newness. What Jesus promised will, indeed, come to pass. A witness to hope fulfilled by the resurrection, Mary hastens to bring hope to the others, a prophet of the possibility of newness in the world of God.

Discernment does not end with the entrance into a religious order. It becomes a way of living day to day, a prayerful form of decision making that allows God's presence to be felt in both big and small actions. Supported by daily prayer and contemplation, the life of a religious is shaped by listening to the voice of God. The many facets of God's voice, and the many ways we hear it, are discussed in chapter 3 on obedience. As human beings live and choose and act, our decisions become habits, and our habits (especially our virtues) help us to make good decisions more easily. One must

---

11. See Walter Brueggemann, *The Prophetic Imagination* (Minneapolis: Fortress, 2001), chap. 4.

commit oneself daily to prayer and discernment, which might at first seem awkward and gradually becomes more natural. Discernment becomes integrated into daily life and the path before us becomes clearer, though the need for prayer and companionship does not end.

Together: The Role of Community in Prophetic Witness

As noted, God's creation of human beings included woman as a response to man's need for companionship. Human beings are created to be communal, to live and work among other human beings. This, too, is a reflection of our *imago Dei*—God, Trinity of Persons, always acts as one. All humans need contact with others, and all Christians are called to live and minister in ways that contribute to the greater human family. Because they do not take spouses or form nuclear families of their own, religious men and women seek out community life in another way.

Community is one of the characteristics that defines religious life. Jesus's ministry was done in community, though his solitude is also noted in the gospels. He gathers like-minded people to accompany him on his path, and they share in his mission to spread the good news of the kingdom, carrying on that task after his death. Community in religious life has multiple meanings. The term "community" can be used to refer to one's congregation, or it can indicate a local household. Beyond the community of religious, it might also be used to refer to the neighborhood in which we live or the parish in which we worship. In this discussion on community living, the focus will first be on community as congregation, and then it will move to community as household in which religious share space, daily life, prayers, meals, and perhaps also ministry.

The decision to enter a particular religious community often revolves around finding "home" with them: attraction to the charism and the types of ministry that community does, plus a resonance between the individual's personality, priorities, and character with those of the congregation as a whole. When all is well, the individual and the congregation are mutually enriched by one another, and the resonance of the individual with the congregation continues to enliven both sides. Congregations, by welcoming new members, must acknowledge that each new member will help shape their future, and individuals allow themselves to be formed by the congregation. The congregation becomes the community in which the individual expresses his or her call to union with God and participation in Jesus's ministry. Like the group that surrounded Jesus, the religious congregation provides a supportive community with a common goal and shared values. Additionally, the corporate action of a group of people multiplies the effect of each individual, helping move forward the kingdom of God here on earth.

Typically, the congregation as a whole is not the community in which an individual lives each day. For most religious congregations today, small household communities of various sizes are the norm. In certain congregations of women, it is typical for households to consist of one or two members, while in others the norm is three to five. Still others live in institutional-type convent communities of many more. Obviously, these differences are going to affect how one lives each day and how relationships between individuals develop within the community context. Yet, for those who live in groups, some general characteristics can be noted.

First, community helps each one live the mission daily, with support from those who know his or her daily realities, joys, and struggles. Second, the daily interaction between community members allows each one to grow in self-awareness, as it is apparent how one's actions affect others. Daily interactions reveal areas for growth. Third, living in groups involves breaking bread together, creating a real union among people who are from different backgrounds and who have different gifts. This union echoes the companionship among Jesus and his disciples, who broke bread, shared stories and material needs, prayed for one another, and carried each other's burdens.

In both the congregation as a whole and the small local community, religious men and women choose a home, a place where they become part of the common story and witness to a life in union with others.

The Necessary Foundation of Prayer

This life dedicated to the imitation of Christ relies on a solid foundation of prayer and contemplation. We learn from Jesus himself the importance of spending time alone with God, away from the need and service to which our vocation calls. Jesus went to pray throughout the gospels, often following time spent ministering to others. At the moment of his greatest spiritual suffering, he led his friends to the Garden of Gethsemane, where he prayed in agony, knowing the suffering that was to come to him. Like Jesus, we must turn our attention to God and to our relationship with God, whether in the ordinary moments of our ministry, the times of great joy, or the times of complete suffering. "The members of each institute, therefore, ought to seek God before all else, and solely; they should join contemplation, by which they cleave to God by mind and heart, to apostolic love, by which they endeavor to be associated with the work of redemption and to spread the kingdom of God."[12] Our prayer and contemplation allow us to know where God is leading and to recall the overwhelming love of God that gives us the strength to follow even when the path is rocky.

12. *Perfectae Caritatis* (Decree on the Up-to-Date Renewal of Religious Life) 5.

Prayer and contemplation become the foundation of our witness. "This is a listening that transforms us and makes us proclaimers and witnesses of the intentions of God in history and of his efficacious activity for salvation."[13] In prayer we come to know Jesus more intimately, to see his face and his ways. In this way, we then discern what it means to follow his path, in this time and place, with the unique gifts each one brings. Mission is imbued with meaning given by its union with the work of Jesus. "Without prolonged moments of adoration, of prayerful encounter with the word, of sincere conversation with the Lord, our work easily becomes meaningless."[14] Prayer allows the love of God to enter the heart and enliven the religious with courage and energy to continue the task of the mission. In *Evangelii Gaudium*, Pope Francis states, "The primary reason for evangelizing is the love of Jesus which we have received, the experience of salvation which urges us to ever greater love of him. What kind of love would not feel the need to speak of the beloved, to point him out, to make him known? If we do not feel an intense desire to share this love, we need to pray insistently that he will once more touch our hearts. We need to implore his grace daily, asking him to open our cold hearts and shake up our lukewarm and superficial existence" (264).

Conclusion

These three elements—discernment, community, and prayer—are fundamental to the vowed life, but they are not in themselves what define it. As we progress through the three vows of obedience, poverty, and celibacy, we hold onto these three elements

13. CICLSAL, "Keep Watch," 7.

14. Pope Francis, *Apostolic Exhortation Evangelii Gaudium: The Joy of the Gospel* (Washington, DC: USCCB, 2013), 262.

as both support for the vowed life and the direction that leads it to its goal of fulfillment and happiness. Over these three rests the element of prophetic witness, which both critiques the contemporary reality in our world and offers a vision for improvement. The prophetic vision of obedience, poverty, and celibacy reorders the priorities of society so that they reflect the desires of God for the human race.

CHAPTER TWO

Vowed Life: Coherence of the Three Vows

Introduction

Like the first followers of Jesus in the gospels, men and women who enter religious life today, called to a profound relationship with Jesus, place their whole lives at the feet of God, seeking a meaningful path. While this book will articulate the path of consecrated life through its commitment to three vows, this chapter seeks the coherence of the three vows as lived all together. Historical examples of religious life and its precursors illustrate the life of a consecrated religious as one of wholeness and fulfillment, as do church documents. In each example of religious life, the prophetic witness of critique and hope for the future will help paint the picture of the coherent prophetic foundation of today's religious life.

Before Christianity: Prophetic Witness to a Better World

Perhaps the prophets are the first in the written Judeo-Christian tradition to illustrate a life given over to God, often with reluctance. Prophets knew that God's guidance would lead them into distasteful, painful, and dangerous situations, yet they could not but do as God demanded of them. Most often, we think of the prophetic messages of doom and gloom, the clarion call to repent of evil and return to God. Walter Brueggemann's framework for prophetic witness shows such messages as challenges to the social norms of oppression and injustice, the critique that forms the beginning of prophecy. Today, reading the social critique of Isaiah or Amos reveals that little has changed in the oppressive nature of human society. Isaiah (1:16-17) tells the people, "Wash yourselves clean! Put away your misdeeds from before my eyes; cease doing evil; learn to do good. Make justice your aim: redress the wronged, hear the orphan's plea, defend the widow." Amos 2:6-8 is even more specific: "Because they hand over the just for silver, and the poor for a pair of sandals; They trample the heads of the destitute into the dust of the earth, and force the lowly out of the way. Son and father sleep with the same girl, profaning my holy name. Upon garments taken in pledge they recline beside any altar. Wine at treasury expense they drink in their temples." Few of the ills of societies past have been eliminated in today's world.

The Old Testament prophets do not end their message with societal critique. They also offer a vision, fueled by hope and energy, for what the world might look like if we as a human family return to God. Their hope rests not only on the possibility of a better life here and now, but also on their faith in an eternal kingdom ruled by God. As Brueggemann argues, the grief and compassion that calls out the ills of the sociopolitical realm brings a companion message of amazement and hope in what could be, if only we can open our minds and hearts to imagine something different. Complacency arises when nothing is critiqued, judged as unfair or against God's will. Critique allows the spell of despair to be broken and newness to emerge.[1]

---

1. See Walter Brueggemann, "Prophetic Criticizing and the Embrace of Pathos," chap. 3 in *The Prophetic Imagination* (Minneapolis: Fortress, 2001).

The story of Christian life truly begins with Jesus and his followers. Like the Old Testament prophets, Jesus calls attention to the ills of the present moment and to hope and joy in the potential of a better future.[2] He does so in preaching and through presence and ministry. He preaches repentance and conversion, focusing on the mercy and love of a Father God who cares for his children. He hangs out with sinners, prostitutes, tax collectors, the poor, the wealthy, fisherman, the injured, blind, lame, and sick. Simply being present to everyone critiques the societal or political judgment that some people are more important or worthy than others. Jesus ministers through healing those who are ill or possessed by demons, forgiving those who are bound in their sorrow for sin, feeding the hungry, and encouraging the weary. He allows the people to hope, for he shows them a more perfect society, both in the material world and in the world to come. Jesus promises this better world is real.

In the case of both the Old Testament prophets and Jesus, the message is clear: God's desire for the earth and the human population is better than the present reality. Injustices and evils are not welcome in God's kingdom, and each of us who hears this call must do what we can to bring them to an end. The prophets and sometimes Jesus show us their reluctance to call out their friends and neighbors as perpetrators of evil or unjust actions. Prophets are not usually popular, and very often they are rejected and persecuted for challenging the status quo and those who use others to keep their power. "Hope is the refusal to accept the reading of reality which is the majority opinion, and one does that only at great political and existential risk."[3] Yet, the message is one that the prophet cannot ignore.

---

2. Pope Francis speaks of the role of Christians in seeking out a better future in *Let Us Dream: The Path to a Better Future* (New York: Simon & Schuster, 2020).

3. Brueggemann, *Prophetic Imagination,* 65.

Religious men and women are called to the witness of prophecy, even though many do not want to claim to speak God's truth. It seems to be boastful, as if saying "I know what God wants to tell you." However, with or without words, religious life speaks prophecy by living with integrity in a way that challenges the inequities of the world and opens the imagination to a new world in which the dream of God for creation is more closely lived out. Witnessing to a new world of greater justice and freedom does not mean consecrated religious are perfect saints all the time—far from it. Striving to make things better does not result in a removal of the human tendency to make mistakes.

Each of the three vows will be taken up as challenges to the status quo separately. Here, it is important to witness that living consecrated life speaks to fulfillment that is real, true, and eternal—one that seeks out meaning and purpose, with hope for a glorious future here on earth and later in heaven, rather than fleeting happiness, found in power, pleasure, and possessions.

Responding to God's Call

Those who enter religious life have experienced a divine call that leads to a path of following Jesus in a more radical way. Our shared Catholic history provides us with many examples of how that path could be lived out. The earliest followers of Jesus were, of course, his apostles. In the Acts of the Apostles, we read of their life together, in which shared possessions, worship, and mission were the characteristics that marked them as Christians even before such a word was used. When Jesus was crucified, his friends and disciples gathered together in fear. With his resurrection, their fears were set aside and replaced with hope and joy, acknowledging the fidelity of God's promise to them, that he would rise again, and in so doing, conquer sin and death. Their lives fundamentally changed by this act of love, the disciples continued to build their community, sharing this experience and witnessing further the work of God in the actions of the resurrected Jesus.

At the beginning of the Acts of the Apostles (chapter 2), we find the apostles gathered together with people of all nations. This is the moment of Pentecost, when the Spirit of God fills the hearts of those faithful ones, uniting them as one Body in all of their difference and drawing them into the great design God offers those who follow him. Peter declares the words of the psalm as a witness to the power of seeking out God's will to follow Jesus: "I saw the Lord ever before me, with him at my right hand I shall not be disturbed. Therefore my heart has been glad and my tongue has exulted; my flesh, too, will dwell in hope, because you will not abandon my soul to the netherworld, nor will you suffer your holy one to see corruption. You have made known to me the paths of life; you will fill me with joy in your presence" (Acts 2:25-28; cf. Ps 16:8-11). Peter clearly knows deep joy and hope, even after the suffering he has experienced, and in his own sinfulness.

This prophetic witness to joy, a joy which comes from the hope of eternal salvation, is the central tenet of faith upon which the vows of poverty, chastity, and obedience rest. The disciples, with joy and hope in their hearts, "devoted themselves to the teaching of the apostles and to the communal life, to the breaking of bread and to the prayers. . . . They ate their meals with exultation and sincerity of heart, praising God and enjoying favor with all the people" (Acts 2:42, 46-47a). This vision of community became the foundation of the earliest monastic communities, together with Acts 4:32, "The community of believers was of one heart and one mind." St. Augustine, writing in the early fifth century, created a rule for men or women living communally.[4] The first line of the Rule is Acts 4:32. He goes on to describe a simple community

---

4. Augustine, *The Monastic Rules*, trans. Agatha Mary and Gerald Bonner (Hyde Park, NY: New City Press, 2004).

lifestyle in which life and possessions are shared in common, rules are laid out for the simplicity of life and for the good of all members of the community, and a routine of shared prayers forms the basis of a common contemplative life. This rule, known as the Rule of St. Augustine, continues to be used today by some religious orders, most notably those in the Dominican family.

The most famous rule of monastic life is that of St. Benedict of Nursia, written in 516.[5] His Rule, like that of St. Augustine, has withstood the test of time because of its adaptability and simplicity. Both rules meet the needs of a variety of people without becoming onerous for the typical religious. In both rules, the goal of union with God was to be achieved by turning away from the desires of the world and converting one's desire to the love of Christ, in a community united by the common life and shared prayer. Benedict articulates this clearly in the prologue to the Rule: "Therefore we intend to establish a school for the Lord's service. In drawing up its regulations, we hope to set down nothing harsh, nothing burdensome. The good of all concerned, however, may prompt us to a little strictness in order to amend faults and to safeguard love. . . . As we progress in this way of life and in faith, we shall run on the path of God's commandments, our hearts overflowing with the inexpressible delight of love. . . . We shall through patience share in the sufferings of Christ that we may deserve also to share in his kingdom. Amen" (RB Prol. 45-46, 49-50).

The monastic form of religious life, modeled on Benedict's Rule, dominated until the dawn of the thirteenth century and the emergence of the mendicant orders. Sts. Francis of Assisi and Dominic envisioned a new way to follow Jesus, one that was not caught up in the monastic tradition's separation from the world. While monks took a vow of stability, by which

5. Timothy Fry, ed., *The Rule of Saint Benedict 1980* (Collegeville, MN: Liturgical Press, 1981).

they meant to live in one monastery for their whole lives, Franciscans and Dominicans adopted itinerancy, modeled on the idea that "the Son of Man has nowhere to rest his head" (Matt 8:20). At a moment when monastic communities had accumulated rather a lot of wealth, the mendicants entered the scene and eschewed a stable home. The Franciscans were the first to use the evangelical counsels of poverty, chastity, and obedience as religious vows.

Expressions of religious life continued to shift and change as new needs emerged and were recognized. The Society of Jesus was founded by St. Ignatius of Loyola in 1540, with particular focus on education and mission. The Ursulines were founded by St. Angela Merici in 1572 as the first religious order dedicated to the education of girls. In the same century, the first non-cloistered group of women religious was founded by St. Louise de Marillac with St. Vincent de Paul in 1633; the Daughters of Charity focused their ministry on the needs of the poor and works of mercy. Following these first foundations, religious orders continued to be founded and renewed in order to meet whatever needs emerged in the world. Regardless of the specific form, charism, and ministry undertaken by particular religious orders, the goal is always to imitate Christ by following the path he laid out for his followers. While some orders focus their identity and activity on exterior actions, others focus on the spiritual union with God that Christians must seek. Both are necessary, just as in Scripture Jesus directs his followers to act on behalf of others as well as to pray to God. In fact, it would be false to assert that these activities are exclusive. Take, for instance, the Ignatian imperative to be a "contemplative in action." Ignatius sought to bring the contemplative foundation of religious life into the world, where preaching and mission belong. Far from separating one element of life from another, we are each called to live in an integral way, so that our external actions and our internal dispositions are part of the same story.

So, too, with religious life. Although we can speak of the counsels individually as needed for deeper understanding, the life consecrated to these vows must hold them all together in one. The witness of previous centuries shows how the evangelical counsels proved useful for shaping Christian living and at the same time allowed for a great diversity of expression as the world changed. This ability to recognize both the value of the historical witness and the importance of engaging in the needs of the modern world is articulated well in *Perfectae Caritatis* (Decree on the Up-to-Date Renewal of Religious Life): "Lay religious life, for men and for women, is a state for the profession of the evangelical counsels which is complete in itself. The holy synod holds it in high esteem, for it is so useful to the Church in the exercise of its pastoral duty of educating the young, caring for the sick, and in its other ministries. It confirms the members in their vocation and urges them to adapt their life to modern requirements" (10). Thus, it seems the core identity of religious life lies not in the ministry of the congregations' members, but rather in their identity with Christ, poor, chaste, and obedient, in whatever work prayer and discernment leads to.

Wholeness of Life under Vows

Consecration by vow to God is constitutive of the religious life, as it unites the religious woman or man with Christ, in his poverty, chastity, and obedience. "Religious vows are . . . an expression of the fact that God has already taken hold of me with a grip so strong and mysterious that I cannot turn away."[6] The evangelical counsels, the content of the vows, however, are calls to all baptized Christians to live out their baptismal call

6. Donald Senior, "Living in the Meantime: Biblical Foundations for Religious Life," in *Living in the Meantime: Concerning the Transformation of Religious Life*, ed. Paul J. Philibert (Mahwah, NJ: Paulist, 1994), 55–57.

by following Jesus. As was discussed in chapter 1, the Second Vatican Council affirmed the universal call to holiness: it is not priests and religious alone who are called to holy life, but rather all Christians. The evangelical counsels offer a model for this holy life. John Paul II in *Vita Consecrata* articulates that "all those reborn in Christ are called to live out, with the strength which is the Spirit's gift, the chastity appropriate to their state of life, obedience to God and to the Church, and a reasonable detachment from material possessions: for all are called to holiness, which consists in the perfection of love."[7] These characteristics of Christ's life help Christians to fulfill the dream of God for all of us, for "they proclaim the liberty of the children of God and the joy of living according to the evangelical beatitudes."[8] Through imitating Christ in all ways, Christians embrace a vision for the world that mirrors God's vision for all creation. All Christians are called to challenge social norms that place love of power, possessions, or self above love of God and neighbor. As Pope Francis stated, "Life exists where there is bonding, communion, fraternity; and life is stronger than death when it is built on true relationships and bonds of fidelity. On the contrary, there is no life when we claim to be self-sufficient and live as islands: in these attitudes, death prevails."[9] Christians are called to declare the reality of life in a world that places false gods above life. In

7. John Paul II, *Vita Consecrata* (Vatican City: Libreria Editrice Vaticana, 1996), 30, http://w2.vatican.va/content/john-paul-ii/en/apost_exhortations/documents/hf_jp-ii_exh_25031996_vita-consecrata.html.

8. CICLSAL, "Starting Afresh from Christ: A Renewed Commitment to Consecrated Life in the Third Millennium" (Vatican City: Libreria Editrice Vaticana, 2002), 13, https://www.vatican.va/roman_curia/congregations/ccscrlife/documents/rc_con_ccscrlife_doc_20020614_ripartire-da-cristo_en.html, 13.

9. *Angelus* (November 10, 2019): *L'Osservatore Romano*, November 11–12, 2019, 8. Quoted in *Fratelli Tutti* 87. Pope Francis, *Fratelli Tutti: Encyclical Letter on Fraternity and Social Friendship* (Vatican City: Libreria Editrice Vaticana, 2020).

Evangelii Gaudium Pope Francis asserts, "I am interested only in helping those who are in thrall to an individualistic, indifferent and self-centered mentality to be freed from those unworthy chains and to attain a way of living and thinking which is more humane, noble and fruitful, and which will bring dignity to their presence on this earth" (208).

While all Christians are called to follow Christ, consecration deepens the call to the evangelical counsels in the person of the religious. Rejecting anything foreign to God's will, religious are called to live more completely out of a love of God that allows the will to unite to God's. "By [the vows, religious] have dedicated their whole lives to [God's] service. . . . Religious, therefore, faithful to their profession and leaving all things for Christ's sake . . . , should follow him, regarding this as the one thing that is necessary. . . . [They] ought to seek God before all else, and solely" (*Perfectae Caritatis 5*). The CICLSAL document "Starting Afresh from Christ" states that the vows confer "radicalness as a response to love."[10] The radical nature of consecration deepens the initial baptismal call to follow Christ, so that the religious man or woman lives transformed, a witness to the limitations of our world and the hope and joy that emerge when one focuses on the kingdom of God.[11] As such, religious consecration involves an asceticism, a self-denial that corresponds to total self-gift out of love. This asceticism removes other obligations, such as are necessary in family life, and the impulse for personal success so common in our culture. Freed of these constraints, the religious man or woman can live more focused on imitating the incarnation, passion, and death of Jesus.

The removal of "earthly cares" accomplished by consecration leads to greater freedom to follow Christ. By the bond of the vows,

10. CICLSAL, "Starting Afresh from Christ," 22.
11. CICLSAL, 33.

he consecrates himself wholly to God, his supreme love. In a new and special way he makes himself over to God, to serve and honor him. True, as a baptized Christian he is dead to sin and dedicated to God; but he desires to derive still more abundant fruit from the grace of his baptism. For this purpose, he makes profession in the Church of the evangelical counsels. He does so for two reasons: first, in order to be set free from hindrances that could hold him back from fervent charity and perfect worship of God, and secondly, in order to consecrate himself in a more thoroughgoing way to the service of God. (LG 44)

This is to share in Christ's self-emptying, the kenosis of he who became human and died on the cross out of love for us.

Consecration by vow is a lifelong all-encompassing commitment to religious life that by definition removes the possibility of other choices. Commitment as such is viewed in the world as something constraining that removes freedom. Instead, commitment allows greater freedom in making the choice for life, a way to find meaning and connection in the world. The commitment of vowed life binds religious men and women to live the will of God to the best of their ability. The will of God is always human joy and fulfillment, the meaning and purpose of life, which Christians find through making the gospel our guide.[12] Our commitments tie us in relationship to others inextricably. Our primary commitments allow us greater freedom within them, greater possibility as we explore the depth of reality present in those commitments. Without committing our lives in such a way, the open possibilities that might be explored draw our attention and take our energy so that relating to others cannot approach

---

12. Howard Gray, "Freedom and Discernment: A Life-Long Pilgrimage," *Human Development* 37 (Summer 2017): 6–15.

the depth for which we long.[13] Commitment allows us to put down roots in order to grow.[14] From the rootedness of our commitments, meaning and growth emerge—"without commitment, freedom is impossible"[15]—not the so-called freedom of endless options, but rather the freedom of self-expression and growth, always with meaning and purpose. We are then free to be transformed, as happens when one turns over her whole being to God's will, to be guided by the life-giving spirit and to grow in abundance. In the words of Karl Rahner, "Freedom is not the capacity for indefinite revision, for always doing something different, but . . . the capacity that creates something final, something irrevocable and eternal."[16]

This commitment of religious to follow the gospel through lifelong vows then plants seeds in the life of the church. *Perfectae Caritatis* states: "Under the impulse of love, which the Holy Spirit pours into their hearts . . . , they live more and more for Christ and for his Body, the Church. . . . The more fervently, therefore, they join themselves to Christ by this gift of their whole life, the fuller does the Church's life become and the more vigorous and fruitful its apostolate" (1). Thus, the gift of self of religious witnesses the power of the Holy Spirit and benefits the church and world as a whole. "All the members of the Church should unflaggingly fulfil the duties of their Christian calling. The profession of the evangelical counsels shines before them as a sign which can and should effectively inspire them to do so. For the People of God has here no lasting city but seeks the city which is to come, and

---

13. Sandra Schneiders, *Selling All: Commitment, Consecrated Celibacy, and Community in Catholic Religious Life* (New York: Paulist, 2001), 91.

14. Image of commitment as rootedness comes from John C. Haughey, "Freedom and Commitment," *The Way* 15, no. 2 (April 1975): 117.

15. Haughey, "Freedom and Commitment," 111.

16. Karl Rahner, *Grace in Freedom* (New York: Herder and Herder, 1969), quoted in Haughey, 113.

the religious state of life, in bestowing greater freedom from the cares of earthly existence on those who follow it, simultaneously reveals more clearly to all believers the heavenly goods which are already present in this age, witnessing to the new and eternal life which we have acquired through the redemptive work of Christ" (LG 44).

Consecration to the evangelical counsels, as it is an extension of the baptismal call of all Christians, is a sign of fidelity enlivening the whole church. Beyond a personal relationship and commitment to Jesus, consecration is expressed through dedication to others here on this earth. The expression of consecration to the evangelical counsels occurs in the mission and work of the religious, striving to make God's kingdom "present here and now through the spirit of the Beatitudes, a spirit capable of giving rise in human society to effective aspirations for justice, peace, solidarity, and forgiveness" (*Vita Consecrata* 27). Religious life as such is an expression of the promise of the gospel in the world here and now.

Eschatology of the Vowed Life

Consecrated life is a witness to the fidelity of God's promise both for a better earthly world and eternity hereafter. Witnessing the gospel message on earth is fundamental to imitating Christ and following the Beatitudes, but consecrated religious life also witnesses to the hope for eternal life in the kingdom of God. Religious life must show the world that there is something beyond the here and now, something, Someone who seeks us as much as we long for him. To live conformed to Christ is "an all-encompassing commitment which foreshadows the eschatological perfection" as far as we can in this time and place (*Vita Consecrata* 16). By consecration to God, religious live out the Christian belief that fulfillment does not come on this earth, no matter how much power we have, our wealth and possessions, or the quality and quantity of our human relationships. None of those things can bring us to the eternal joy God offers. The power, possessions, and relationships we have are gifts of God; consecration offers those gifts back to God for the good of the world. Religious life witnesses to a world in which the gifts we have are offered for the common good, as a means to promote human dignity among everyone, especially those who are most marginalized. As Pope Francis states in *Fratelli Tutti*, "Human beings are so made that they cannot live, develop, and find fulfillment except in the sincere gift of self to others."[17]

Our hope comes not only from the belief that this world can be more hospitable and more human, but also from the utter faith that God's dream will be fulfilled in all eternity. *Vita Consecrata* speaks to the eschatological dimension of religious life as "a foreshadowing of the future kingdom" (26). Religious life, for all the asceticism and self-gift it calls for, witnesses the hope for fulfillment in the world to come, a "total transformation" of human existence in eternal union with Christ and the Father. It is a recognition that here on earth we are pilgrims longing for the transcendent life of God, eager to be filled with God's spirit in heaven. Living as Christians, we know and witness to the fact that there is deeper meaning to life and that we are connected as human beings to the transcendent God even as we live here on earth without easily recognizing our connections. As quoted above, *Lumen Gentium* (44) articulates the role of the religious life in witnessing to the kingdom of God in the here and now, a witness to the pilgrimage all human beings share on this earth, journeying always toward our eternal life in God.

In *Vita Consecrata*, Pope John Paul II draws together the two sources of hope to be found in religious life—the hope

---

17. Pope Francis, *Fratelli Tutti: Encyclical Letter on Fraternity and Social Friendship* (Vatican City: Libreria Editrice Vaticana, 2020), 87.

of a present world growing in configuration to God's desire for it, and the hope of a future world in the hereafter, where we are united with God. "By this profound 'configuration' to the mystery of Christ, the consecrated life brings about in a special way that *confessio Trinitatis* which is the mark of all Christian life; it acknowledges with wonder the sublime beauty of God, Father, Son, and Holy Spirit, and it bears joyful witness to his loving concern for every human being" (16).

Consecration by the vows offers a prophetic witness to Christian faith in a future that is good, beautiful, and ordained by God. It is witness to the gospel's message of reconciliation and mercy. Pope Francis, in *Evangelii Gaudium* states, "The Gospel has an intrinsic principle of totality: it will always remain good news until it has been proclaimed to all people, until it has healed and strengthened every aspect of humanity, until it has brought all men and women together at table in God's kingdom. The whole is greater than the part" (234–37). In religious life, men and women seek to make the universality of the gospel message a concrete reality here and now, and to offer hope for a world to come. As articulated by Donald Senior and others, religious life is an expression of "living in the meantime," a time between the present and the future, from the faith foundation that strives to bring about this ideal we believe in.[18] Religious live this tension with intentionality as a sign of hope and possibility in the church and the world.

Conclusion

By carrying on the traditions of religious throughout Christian history as well as the lifestyle of Old Testament prophets, religious life today challenges the status quo and brings hope

18. Senior, "Living in the Meantime," 55–71.

and joy to the world. Consecrating their lives to obedience, poverty, and celibacy, women and men religious witness to the power of God alive and working in our world. The three vows together allow a complete self-gift, one which brings freedom and devotion to ameliorate the needs of the world. "As a response to the gift of God, the vows are a triple expression of a single 'yes' to the one relationship of total consecration."[19] We now turn to examine each of the vows separately, beginning with the vow of obedience.

19. Sacred Congregation for Religious and for Secular Institutes, "Essential Elements in the Church's Teaching on Religious Life as Applied to Institutes Dedicated to Works of the Apostolate" (Vatican City: Libreria Editrice Vaticana, 1983), 14, http://www.vatican.va/roman_curia/congregations/ccscrlife /documents/rc_con_ccscrlife_doc_31051983_magisterium-on-religious-life _en.html.

CHAPTER THREE

The Vow of Obedience

Introduction

The centrality of mission—following in the footsteps of Jesus to spread his prophetic message of grief and hope—is clearly the defining external feature of religious life today, while contemplation and prayer imbue all elements of consecrated life. Jesus followed the will of God the Father to his own death. Leading to that moment, Jesus drew people to himself, asking them to follow where he led and do as he did. Jesus had a uniquely close relationship with God his own Father, a relationship that we may attempt to imitate but will never quite achieve. How, then, do women and men today seek out and follow the will of God? Like Jesus, we must embrace a call to obey the will of God in our life. This obedience, as it was with Jesus, must be built on a foundation of mutual trust, in which I know that God's will is never going to harm, but rather will lead to joy and the fullness of being. "To seek the will of God means to seek a friendly and benevolent will, which desires our fulfillment, that desires, above all, a free response in love to its love, in order to make of us instruments of divine love."[1] Without the foundation

---

1. CICLSAL, "*Faciem tuam, Domine, requiram*: The Service of Authority and Obedience" (Vatican City: Libreria Editrice Vaticana, 2008), 4,

45

of prayer and interior life, in which I know deeply that God loves me and supports me, and that God wants my eternal happiness, my freedom to obey is curtailed. With this prayerful foundation, I can open my heart to seek out and do the will of God. In that is obedience freely sought and lovingly acted upon.

The vow of obedience is typically listed third among the three vows, yet here it is addressed first for multiple reasons. It is a difficult concept, particularly in today's Western world, which focuses so much on the needs of the individual and his or her freedom to make decisions about his or her life. Thus, obedience puts us face-to-face with the countercultural nature of religious life. Second, obedience is perhaps the most misunderstood and maligned of the three vows of religious life. Because it stands in contrast to the liberty valued in society, it challenges our concept of happiness and what is right or not right. It also has become a concept that places us in submission to people who have more authority, thus challenging the equality we seek in society. When misused, or misunderstood, it can make one group or person subservient to others in a way that denies their maturity or humanity. Finally, obedience is addressed first because for some orders it is the only vow made, understood in such a way that poverty and chastity are included in it. Thus, obedience can be considered the overarching vow that in itself implies and includes the others.

In past centuries, obedience was clear and easy to understand. When common belief held that society as a whole was properly ordered in a hierarchy, as it was for centuries and continues to be in some societies, obedience meant knowing your place in social and familial hierarchy and obeying the norms attached to it. Those who were your "betters" or superiors were to be obeyed, and most people also had other

---

http://www.vatican.va/roman_curia/congregations/ccscrlife/documents /rc_con_ccscrlife_doc_20080511_autorita-obbedienza_en.html.

levels in the hierarchy beneath them. In the Western world, women were usually subjected to the power of their fathers or husbands, or their grown male children. At the top of the social hierarchy was the king and the pope, and regularly throughout history they argued over which of them was subject to the other. Everyone else fell into line below those two.

Theologians understood hierarchy to be divinely decreed. The world made sense when it was contained in its proper order: just as creation occurred over six days, forming order out of chaos in a particular sequence, so too the social order kept humanity from falling back into chaos. Catastrophes and problems were caused by the world literally becoming disordered. Thus, the concept of obedience ensured that the world remained good and holy, people (and everything that exists) were well-established in clear-cut categories of existence, and all remained as God had ordained it to be. The disorder of unclear stations in life mirrored the chaos of the waters of Genesis before God calmed them: "and the earth was without form or shape, with darkness over the abyss and a mighty wind sweeping over the waters" (Gen 1:2). Disorder would surely lead to tempests.

The church and religious congregations have an ordered hierarchical structure that reflects past social hierarchies. Church hierarchy is centered on ordination and the different levels of ordination, with a clear demarcation between ordained and nonordained. Monastic orders traditionally ranked members first by their duties or offices and then as individuals by seniority. The proper order was known and followed, and responsibilities were assigned according to the community's monastic rule. Their behavior, actions, and even order of seating in chapel and refectory were clearly spelled out. Clarity of hierarchy and rank has the advantage of eliminating questions of propriety and obedience. Doing what is right is simply a matter of following established rules and the decrees of superiors.

While societies retain some hierarchical structures, those structures have been questioned and many are dismantled. With greater acknowledgment of socioeconomic inequalities over the last few years, the role of such formal norms in perpetuating social sin brings them under further scrutiny. This shift from focusing on black-and-white rules governing obedience and moral questions highlights the need for a well-formed conscience to tackle moral questions and a life of discernment and prayer to address the questions of obedience in religious and Christian life.

Religious orders today exemplify every type of hierarchy possible within the church. Canon law requires that congregations designate persons to be superiors over their membership, who are ultimately responsible for the order as a whole. Today, among women's religious orders in the United States, most congregations focus on discernment, both personal and communal, as a source of obedience rather than hierarchy and structure. Thus, this chapter will examine obedience in terms of the duty and vow of the individual religious to seek out and follow the will of God in everyday life largely without external guidelines such as rules or the command of religious superiors that bypass the exercise of an individual's conscience. Thus, the focus remains within the context of theological anthropology: the human mind, in the image and likeness of God, has the capacity to think, engage in learning, and act according to its will.

This chapter begins with a theological exploration of obedience in the life of Jesus and in his teaching. Then, we explore obedience as discernment of the will of God, next as obedience to the charism (and thus to the identity of the individual religious), obedience to community life, obedience within the context of the church, and obedience to the needs of the world. Taken together, these aspects give us a fuller understanding of the vow of obedience in today's world. The chapter concludes by situating the vow and practice of obedience within the prophetic witness to the joy of Christianity that religious life offers to the world.

Obedience in the Life of Jesus

Jesus lived entirely in obedience to God the Father. He often speaks of "doing the will of the Father," for example in John 6:38, "I came . . . not to do my own will but the will of the one who sent me" or John 4:34, "My food is to do the will of the one who sent me and to finish his work." Jesus teaches us to pray that our wills, too, be united to God's, and he shows us what that means by his actions of healing, forgiveness, feeding, and compassion. Jesus, in obedience, comes down from heaven to become the Bread of Life that nourishes everyone.

Yet it is in the passion, death, and resurrection that Jesus's will is most obviously united with the Father's will, even in the struggle and pain. Obedience is most tested when following God's desire causes pain. Jesus's struggle is clear in his prayer in the Garden before he is arrested: "My Father, if it is possible, let this cup pass from me; yet, not as I will, but as you will" (Matt 26:39). The agony Jesus bears is palpable as he repeats this prayer, alone with his sleeping friends. Both human and divine, Jesus experiences true human suffering, the sorrow of leaving his friends, the fear of the cross and its pain and death, and he knows the loss and mourning his death will bring to those he loves. He remains obedient to the will of God, for "he was absolutely certain that everything found its meaning in complete fidelity to the plan of salvation willed by the Father."[2] His death, as full of suffering as it was to be, would be an act of love, restoring humanity on the path toward God, lost as we were through sinfulness.

---

2. CICLSAL, *Faciem Tuam*, 5.

The obedience Jesus lives helps us see that there is meaning in suffering, and so we are able to unite our suffering with his. The suffering Jesus experiences is done completely out of love—out of Jesus's love for his friends (us!) and God's love for all of creation. Jesus's obedience to the will of God asserts the goodness of God's will, that it works toward the kingdom, toward God's desire for all of humanity and all of creation. Though obedience calls us to make painful choices and do difficult or sorrowful things, following the will of God means doing so out of faith and hope that the suffering is not to last.

Obedience to God

We have established that human beings are made in God's image and likeness, implanted with a deep desire to become ever closer to God. The incarnation of Jesus marked a significant moment in the human longing for God by uniting humanity and divinity in the one person of Christ. This union, for which human beings strive, turned the tide of sin and death toward reconciliation and eternal life. God's act of love impels us toward union with him in eternity. "Obedience to God is the path of growth, and therefore, of freedom for the person" in that God's plan is always what leads to greater human dignity, to a closer approximation of the dream of God for the human person.[3]

The story of creation also informs us that we are not God. This, as we see in the fall from grace in the Garden of Eden, is the primary tendency to sin: to assume that we are divine ourselves, and that we have a right to something that God has not provided for us. Adam and Eve sinned in disobedience—and their disobedience was a lack of humility and a

3. CICLSAL, 5.

lack of self-knowledge. Our primary obedience is to God, because God created us and provides us with everything we need. "By their profession of obedience, religious offer the full dedication of their own wills as a sacrifice of themselves to God, and by this means they are united more permanently and securely with God's saving will" (*Perfectae Caritatis* 14). That obedience depends on our humility, which means we must possess some self-knowledge, and most especially the knowledge that we cannot do anything without God.

Yet "doing something" is the bare minimum. What God desires of each one of us is to live in joy. How do we know what joy is? How do we follow the path that will lead us to joy? This is where we find obedience: in the discernment that is required to know God's will and the willpower needed to follow it. This discernment is ultimately about finding our joy in the world.

Previously, we spoke of the need for discernment in order to hear the call to follow God, to decide for ourselves by listening to God where we are going and how we are to live this life. Obedience requires that our discernment never ends. We don't just say "yes" once, but we say "yes" over and over again to the demands of our life, to following where our call leads us.

One of the most helpful concepts I have found, and one I truly believe in, comes from Ignatius of Loyola. Ignatius is the great discerner, and his writings and spirit have guided people from all walks of life for five hundred years. In Ignatian spirituality, God's greatest desire for each one of us *is* our greatest desire. The desire planted most deeply in my heart was put there by God, and so our desires—mine and God's—coalesce to bring fulfillment to my life in the same way that they bring fulfillment to the dreams God has for me. That is the theological way of saying that what makes me most happy is exactly what God wants for me. God's joy and my joy are one.

Of course, it's not as easy as that. As human beings, we can easily be distracted from what really brings joy by things that bring us temporary pleasure. We can also be blinded by distractions that lead us down different paths, or by our sinfulness that we must later make account for. For this reason, a lively prayer life, a grateful heart, and a support system are needed to help us keep our egos in check.

How do we know what God calls us to? We know by listening to our hearts, by listening to the spirit work in us, by listening to those who know us, and by hearing the cries of the world around us. There is an old saying that we should pray with the Bible in one hand and the newspaper in the other. I would add to that the attention we place within ourselves to sense what pulls us internally. I might feel a real draw to work for the needs of the people seeking asylum on our borders. Yet, my response to that draw must be in line with the teachings of Jesus and also in line with my own gifts and talents. I may *want* to help them with their legal status, but if I have no foreign language skills or knowledge of immigration law, I am little help in that arena. My discernment might then lead me to other ways to be of service (collecting donations, educating people where I live, or communicating Catholic social teaching to my parish) or it may lead me to develop new gifts in myself (by learning Spanish or discerning whether to go to law school).

It must be noted, too, that discernment is about choosing between two good things. When we talk about obedience to God and to the needs of the world, it's clear that the needs are abundant and the path of Jesus is wide and diverse. Obedience may offer us many options, all of them good, and all of them consistent with our own gifts. Discernment then comes into the equation, through which we ask God for guidance in our prayer, that the path that is most right at this moment be shown to us. Obedience, then, calls us to commit our lives wholly to that choice, to live it to its fullest until it is clear that some other need is calling us in a different direction.

Obedience to Order and Charism

Obedience takes on a new form when we have made a commitment to something. Once we have entered a religious order, we also commit to align our life to the order according to its spirituality and charism. Each order has its particular understanding of obedience, and a rule that must be obeyed as well. Thus it is that members of certain orders profess only the one vow of obedience—by it, the religious vows to follow all other customs of the community to the best of his or her ability.

One of the most helpful encounters I had in discernment occurred with a vocations director of an order that I did not join. She got to know me and helped me a great deal, and then one day, after talking for several months, she said to me that it was clear I am called to be a teacher. I agreed that this is definitely clear to me. She then said that her congregation does not teach, and so I should discern with other groups. While I felt a draw to that congregation, I also knew that teaching was so central to my very being that leaving it behind would not fulfill me. She was calling me to recognize that obedience to their charism would not allow me to follow God's call for me.

Each order must follow its charism. The particular charism of each congregation represents the vision of the founder or foundress for the order. It comes from the recognition of a particular need in the church or the world that is not adequately being met. Charisms might be likened to personalities. There are many in the world, and no one is better than another, yet each one of us has our own particular personality. Like someone who is seeking out a life partner, women and men seeking religious life look for the charism that is most compatible with their own and most likely to allow personal growth and increasing holiness. The charism of a congregation never changes, though it might need to be expressed differently in word and ministry as the world changes. Again, the analogy of a personality is helpful: at root, our personalities remain the same, but different characteristics are drawn out of us at different times of our lives or with different companions. I am an introvert, and when I'm in groups of people I don't know I'm likely to be rather quiet; on the other hand, with friends I am a lively conversationalist. I am still me, yet I might express myself very differently in different contexts. My congregation's charism of discovering and revealing the love of God is expressed differently among children in our academies than it is among migrants with whom we minister.

The world in which we live today is in a constant state of change. As the needs of the world shift, so too does the expression of charism. Obedience calls us to be open to change as a way to continue to meet the needs of God's people. Most congregations today have been marked by monumental changes in the twentieth century. Those changes shaped our sisters and their development as women religious, yet the world has not stopped moving under our feet. Our shared obedience calls us as congregations to keep listening to what the world needs and to seek out a way to meet the need through new expressions of our charism. "If each of you is a precious opportunity for others to meet with God, it is about rediscovering the responsibility of being prophetic as a community, to seek together, with humility and patience, a word of sense that can be a gift for the country and for the Church, and to bear witness to it with simplicity. You are like antennas ready to receive the smallest innovations prompted by the Holy Spirit, and you can help the ecclesial community to take on this gaze of goodness and find new and bold ways to reach all peoples."[4]

4. Pope Francis, "Audience with Participants at the Encounter Organized by the Italian Conference of Secular Institutes," Rome, May 10, 2014, quoted in CICLSAL, "Keep Watch! To Consecrated Men and Women Journeying in the Footsteps of God" (Vatican City: Libreria Editrice Vaticana, 2014), 13.

Obedience to Life in Community

As illustrated in the creation of Adam and Eve, human beings are meant to be with other human beings. We are not meant to walk our path alone. Jesus, too, reminds us of the need for companionship by surrounding himself with friends and sending them out in pairs. In religious life, because we do not choose to unite ourselves in marriage to another person, our companionship takes the form of community. In committing our lives to apostolic religious life, we also commit ourselves to a type of obedience to community living, which may be one of the most challenging aspects of living as a religious. While we will pick up other elements of community life in other chapters, here we speak to obedience in community.

In discussing obedience to God, we have noted that God wants us to follow our deepest desire for fulfillment and wholeness. Yet, our commitments in this life provide certain checks on our understanding of obedience to God through our own perceptions and preferences. Once we commit to living in community, we commit also to sometimes submitting our desires to the needs or desires of those we live with. The needs of a sister may be more important for my attention than my needs in a particular moment. "Religious, as members of Christ, should live together as brothers and should give pride of place to one another in esteem . . . , carrying one another's burdens. . . . A community gathered together as a true family in the Lord's name enjoys his presence . . . , through the love of God which is poured into their hearts by the Holy Spirit. . . . For love sums up the law . . . and is the bond which makes us perfect . . . ; by it we know that we have crossed over from death to life" (*Perfectae Caritatis* 15). Every day, my discernment about my own actions must take into account the impact they have on others and the needs of those around me—not just in my ministry but also in my household. To be honest, this commitment is usually far less of a burden than it is for friends who have husbands and children: I very rarely get awakened in the middle of the night to attend to someone else's needs.

Being available to help my sisters when they need a ride to the airport or a companion at the doctor's office shows me a glimpse of their vulnerability, and in that, a bit of my own. We are sisters together, and their well-being is part of my (and our) well-being. My congregation focuses on the image of "One Body" to help us grow into the future as an international congregation with many different cultures. By understanding one another and having true compassion, even for those we don't understand, we become more and more united to Christ and the church universal. My household community is just one example of that phenomenon, and one that is much easier for me to grasp and participate in. If I can't be compassionate with someone I see and speak with every day, how can I possibly be united with someone who lives in a place and culture far from my own? CICLSAL puts it well: "The search for the will of God and the willingness to carry it out is the spiritual cement that saves the group from the fragmentation that can arise from the great variety of persons in all their diversity when they are lacking a unifying principle."[5]

Obedience to community can also be "writ large," meaning that it might call us to ministry we don't expect or to places we don't wish to go. One of the sisters I lived with early on spoke of how she had committed herself never to say "no" when the congregation asked her to take on a particular service. This cost her a great deal, especially later in her life when she struggled to discern whether she had the energy to take on one more demanding appointment. To her, this was less of a call of obedience to the congregation than it was an expression of her commitment and gratitude for the gifts

---

5. CICLSAL, *Faciem Tuam*, 18.

she had received. Obedience to community can also be that response of "yes" when you are recognized to be the one at this time to have the gifts the community discerns are needed.

Handing over our lives in obedience to the will of God is indeed incredibly challenging in this moment. Allowing for these moments of commitment to overstep our personal desires or plans requires confidence and trust that our sisters and brothers are listening to the Spirit attentively and that by calling on me they are speaking in God's voice. Let us each trust in that Spirit of call and consolation.

Obedience in the Church

Religious profess obedience in different ways. Jesuits are known for their vow of obedience to the pope, which is a bit more dramatic than most other orders. Yet all orders we are discussing here profess obedience to an institution that is situated within the church and subject to canon law and church doctrine. Thus, the church, too, is a recipient of our obedience. However, like all other forms of obedience, this must be put into a proper context to be understood.

There are certain times when obedience to the church is fairly obvious. At least weekly we proclaim a creed in which we declare what it is we believe about God, Jesus, the Holy Spirit, and the church. The tenets of this creed are non-negotiables for Christians. We cannot profess our Christianity and contradict anything that is expressed in that creed. Our faith also demands of us certain moral imperatives that we must follow, and those again are non-negotiable. This includes, for example, the Ten Commandments, with a fairly clear interpretation of their extension in today's world that is stated in the *Catechism of the Catholic Church*. Of course, our fallen nature means that sometimes we fall short of our ideals, and at that point we ask God for forgiveness.

Amid today's reports of sexual abuse and secrecy scandals among clergy, it is clear to all of us that the church is a human institution. The humanness of the church does not diminish its holiness nor the fact that it is divinely guided. Yet while the Holy Spirit guides, human beings, even prominent clergy, sometimes make incredible and harmful mistakes. That is absolutely without doubt, and perhaps the case of sexual abuse and secrecy is more properly placed within a conversation about reconciliation and healing. Within the context of obedience, it may help us to remember that the church is not just about the members of the hierarchy and their actions, but rather it might be better understood as the people of God.

While obedience is to be held in regard to those with authoritative power in the church (thus the hierarchy), it seems it should always be balanced with the needs of the people of God. We are called, yes, to obey the church as a whole, yet what is to be done when the leaders of the church are inconsistent or seemingly disagree with the needs of the people of God? In this case, my call to obedience to God demands of me a prophetic voice, speaking up for God's will even when that means challenging the church. Often we think of prophecy on the margins of society, with the force of the church's authority behind it (for example, the Nuns on the Bus). For one whose life is committed to the church, it is much more challenging to be a prophetic voice which calls into question the very actions of the church he or she loves. Commitment to the church in obedience also means calling it out, drawing from the church what is right and challenging what is wrong. It means being prophetic, holding up the needs of those on the peripheries and pointing out hypocrisy. It means taking a firm stance against the church's actions when those actions are not of God.

In addition to the obedience of challenging the church, the Catholic faith gives us the imperative of following our personal conscience. Vatican II tells us that personal conscience, when well developed, is the ultimate source of knowledge for each person in discerning his or her actions. Following my conscience does not mean that I do whatever I want. Rather, it means that I know how to distinguish between right and wrong, and I direct my actions to what is right. While this requires discernment, it is a more fundamental level of decision making than discernment. Discernment is often the second step, when I have determined that I have two choices in front of me that are both good; I discern which I think God is calling me to do, allowing God's will to guide me. Following my conscience is the previous step: to determine what is right and what is wrong. If I am faced with one right choice and one wrong choice, my conscience clearly tells me what I should do. Following God never requires me to do something that is evil, and so following my conscience and its voice requires me to do the good. In a way it is much simpler than discernment, for when good and evil are clear, the answer is clear. When discerning between two good options, the choice can be much more difficult.

How does conscience work into obedience? We have many examples in our world today. For many years, the US bishops have been divided on different issues, particularly issues of voting in the context of the US political system. Some bishops have told us that we have to vote against any politician who holds positions in support of the legality of abortion, regardless of other issues that might contradict Catholic teaching. Some bishops tell us that we should decide who to vote for by taking into account all issues on the platform a politician holds (the "seamless garment"), which might lead us to vote for someone who would support abortion's legality but also fight for social justice issues such as care for unwed mothers, care for those who are poor, and the rights of migrants. How do we decide when the path before us does not have a clear answer of what is right? In this case, the guidance of the church hierarchy cannot simply tell us what we should do. Thus, our conscience must determine the most appropriate decision. The US bishops' document *Faithful Citizenship* states, "Catholics may choose different ways to respond to compelling social problems, but we cannot differ on our moral obligation to help build a more just and peaceful world through morally acceptable means, so that the weak and vulnerable are protected and human rights and dignity are defended."[6] This does not mean that each person makes up his or her mind on a whim, but that with a good education, a solid foundation of the facts of Catholic teaching and the political platforms, the individual Catholic votes carefully according to what his or her conscience says is the best choice. The bishops and other authoritative sources offer information that an individual takes into account along with the conscience regarding a particular decision or action: "The judgments and recommendations that we make as bishops on such specific issues do not carry the same moral authority as statements of universal moral teachings. Nevertheless, the Church's guidance on these matters is an essential resource for Catholics as they determine whether their own moral judgments are consistent with the Gospel and with Catholic teaching."[7]

I have left begging the question of disagreement with the moral authority of the church: what if your bishop clearly states that a vote cast for one who supports abortion's legality is sinful, and yet you find your conscience leads you to the opposite conclusion? Church teaching is pretty clear: follow your conscience. Human beings, formed in the image

6. United States Conference of Catholic Bishops, *Forming Consciences for Faithful Citizenship: A Call to Political Responsibility from the Catholic Bishops of the United States* (February 2020), 20, https://www.usccb.org/issues-and-action/faithful-citizenship/upload/forming-consciences-for-faithful-citizenship.pdf.

7. US Conference of Catholic Bishops, *Forming Consciences,* 33.

and likeness of God, can trust that obeying a well-formed conscience will lead to good moral judgments.

Obedience to the Calls of the World

Pope Francis has continually reminded us of the necessity that is both timeless and timely: to attend to the needs of those who are on the peripheries. As religious, we are part of the church institutional—that is part of the definition of our congregational membership. Yet if we remain too comfortable in that institution, we might lose sight of the world. We must always find ourselves on the edges, at the boundaries, with those who are powerless.

The reality is that religious nearly always have more power and resources than those who live on the peripheries. Our call is not to deny that we have power, but to use it in ways that help those who need it, and those who need it are not those who bring us more power or recognition, but those who have nothing of the sort to offer us. Thus our call to obey the needs of the world is a call to remain very cognizant of the gifts we have of influence, wealth, power, and education, and to place all that we have at the disposal of those who do not have it. We must deliberately place ourselves on the peripheries or we lose our purpose on the church.

What does it mean to be at the peripheries? First of all, it means figuratively reading that newspaper. We must look with open eyes on what is happening in the world. We need to be informed, not just of what's happening in our neighborhood—though we should start there—or among local Catholics, or in our congregations' schools or hospitals, but also in the neighborhoods across town, and across the country, and around the world. The peripheries are found in all those places.

Our call is found where the needs we see on the peripheries meet the gifts we have and the desires deep in our hearts.

For some, standing at the peripheries might mean educating the very wealthy in ways that highlight Catholic social teaching, forming them to use their resources for the good of the world. It might mean being kind to an elder who is lonely. It might mean educating others about climate change and how it affects the poorest nations disproportionately. It might mean reaching out to the transgender member of our parish who is being harassed or discriminated against. The peripheries to which each person or religious order is called can be right where the individual is already planted, or it can be around the world. There are incredible examples of commitments made by small congregations in the American Midwest to provide much-needed resources to communities in Africa or Haiti. Likewise, congregations have made dramatic commitments to their local communities and the planet in the immediate surroundings of their motherhouses. There are many ways to be attentive to the needs of those on the peripheries, even if we are limited by our physical location or financial situation. How is the Holy Spirit speaking to us through the world around us, and how can the Spirit help us imagine new ways to meet its ever changing needs?

The people at the peripheries are the most important call of the world around us, and their call is intertwined with the call of our planet. As our world continues to suffer the effects of our consumption and pollution, the people who suffer most are those who are poor and whose voices are not considered in the decision making of powerful governments. As individuals and as a collective of informed and caring women, we are bound by our knowledge of the distress of the world to act in small and large ways for its healing and improvement.

These calls sometimes seem impossibly big, beyond the reach of our littleness. Yet, we live focused on the dream of God for all creation, and we have hope because we trust that God's dream will be fulfilled and the world will be transformed. As we work toward a world that is integrated, we become more aware that all our efforts united can bring God's plan into fulfillment.

Conclusion

Within the history of religious orders, there was long a preoccupation that being in the world would result in corruption, while religious were called to be holy and removed from the world. This led to monasteries establishing themselves in remote places and walling themselves off from the world around them. Gradually the idea of a religious life out in the world grew more common, though never replacing the monastic life that some are still called to. As apostolic religious, we choose to remain always touching the world, responding to its needs, integrating our lives not only in prayer but also in the beauty of what God created. More than ever, this contact with the world puts us in contact with the temptations of materialism, individualism, secularism, and any number of other movements and desires that can distract us from the one true desire deep within our heart. As much as we are called to be at the service of the world, we must also develop a discerning spirit that keeps our eyes on the path before us. With this placement of religious life within the world and yet critical of it, obedience "is living in the time between call and fulfillment, between promise and realization, between the world as we know it and the community of the blessed we hope to join. Obedience reminds us that we are laboring for a kingdom yet to come, for a peace always in process, for a justice always being worked out, for a love still being developed."[8] In this in-between space, religious live a

8. Howard Gray, "Exploring Three Dimensions of the Vow of Obedience," *Horizon* 28, no. 3 (Fall 2003): 9.

prophetic witness to the possibility and hope of what will be when God's reign is fulfilled.

Jesus, always at the center of our call, must remain that center. In practical terms that centeredness is aided by a lively prayer life, the support of a community that can call us back when we stray from our mission, and an attentiveness to the deep desire for God that is both within us and calls us from the world in which we live. While many different sources of authority and obedience face us, the religious must recognize that all are expressions of the one obedience to the call we have received to follow in the path of our Savior.

The call of religious men and women to obedience is one that contradicts the independence and individuality we learn through Western culture. By commitment to obedience to God, church, and community, we profess our desire to hold our individual needs in a wider context, not always to put them first. Rather than focusing on personal success or wealth, obedience calls us to recognize that we have not earned what we have and that the resources we have received must be placed at the service of others. It means deliberately placing ourselves among those who are marginalized rather than among the rich and powerful. Placing our gifts at the feet of others is our prophetic witness to a world that is moving toward God's plan for us. We profess in our obedience that what we have is not ours and that power and privilege do not bring us ultimate joy.

CHAPTER FOUR

The Vow of Poverty

Introduction

The evangelical counsel of poverty is not meant to exalt poverty as desirable, but to show it as a characteristic lived by Jesus. Jesus showed us how poor we are, as dependent on God for all that we need. His actions illustrate the value of life and human dignity over all manner of materialism and prejudice. Pope Francis, in *Evangelii Gaudium,* states, "Our faith in Christ, who became poor, and was always close to the poor and the outcast, is the basis of our concern for the integral development of society's most neglected members" (186). *We are not called to be poor* in terms of material deprivation. Material deprivation is scandalous in Scripture, unjust and degrading, and the faithful are called to mitigate poverty in the world.[1] The call to religious poverty at once redefines poverty and highlights our belief that no one in this world should be materially poor; that is, no one should be denied the necessities for a human life, including food, shelter, medical care, an opportunity to work, access to clean water and proper sanitation, a basic education, and whatever

---

1. Gustavo Gutierrez, *A Theology of Liberation* (Maryknoll, NY: Orbis, 1988), 165.

other material needs are required for a human to live in dignity. Choosing a vow of poverty in no way sanctifies actual material poverty, nor does it eliminate our responsibility to work to end it.

What, then, is this call to poverty, so strong that we make a vow of poverty? If we really believe poverty is an evil to be eradicated, why are we vowing our lives to it? After providing an overview of the meaning of a vow of poverty, this chapter hopes to shed some light on a theological understanding of poverty through the incarnation of God, an examination of how the poverty of the world shapes the vow of poverty, and the role of a spirituality of poverty in consecrated life.

What Is the Vow of Poverty?

Religious men and women make a vow of poverty in such a way that it removes the attachment to and distraction of material possessions. It is a vow to live simply, to disavow the cultural fixation on wealth and possessions as our identity, "caring with sincerity for those who have had less luck in life."[2] By sidestepping this concept of identity through possessions, we recognize the inhumanity of this element of our culture and reclaim the true worth and intrinsic dignity of the human person. "Poverty means being at the service of brothers and sisters, getting involved and serving, living with simplicity, without artificial needs, in harmony with creation and with an awareness that there are millions of human beings who live, or rather, survive with less than what they really need."[3]

2. Pope Francis, *The Strength of Vocation: Consecrated Life Today, a Conversation with Fernando Prado* (Quezon City, Philippines: Claretian Publications, 2018), 83.

3. Francis, *Strength of Vocation*, 83.

The consecrated religious gives up personal ownership of personal possessions on entrance to religious life and continues to hand over all resources throughout life[4] through the particular processes of his or her congregation. By not personally owning anything, the religious also gives up the insecurity of not having enough and the worry over protecting personal possessions. He or she participates in common ownership of all for the benefit of all, trusting that everything needed will be provided for his or her use and that all in the community will receive what they need regardless of what they have to contribute to the whole. A practical result of this common ownership and sharing is to remove the connection between what I have earned and what I can spend. No longer is personal worth or worthiness equated to financial income; additionally, the value of work is not determined by the payment received for it. While work is itself a human right, part of human dignity, one's talents or work abilities should not determine whether one has enough food or proper shelter. "They should, each in his own assigned task, consider themselves bound by the common law of labor, and while by this means they are provided with whatever they need for their sustenance or their work, they should reject all undue solicitude, putting their trust in the providence of the heavenly Father" (*Perfectae Caritatis* 13).

In disavowing personal wealth and ownership, we also recognize that all that we have is gift. Religious women and men generally have more resources available to them than the poorest in the society. Because those resources are recognized as gift, they must be used for the benefit of the society as a whole: thus, religious poverty can also be seen as living simply so that we are good stewards of our resources for the benefit of the whole world. Reliance on God for our needs

---

4. Governed by canon law, each congregation has its own practices and traditions for handing over material possessions.

should not lead us to overconsumption, but rather to use what we need and share what we have in honesty, openness, and simplicity. In doing so, we continue to rely on God to provide for all our needs throughout the changing stages of our lives. We recognize that our role in society goes beyond caring for ourselves alone: our responsibility as Christians is to work toward the kingdom of God.

Sharing what I have is another way of recognizing the dignity of each human person, that each one of us is created in the image and likeness of God. Though I have more resources, my worth is no greater in God's eyes. We know that we do nothing to earn what God gives us and that we are so small and humble—so human—in comparison to the God we believe in. This is our real poverty, and with this concept of the humility of the human person, all of us are equal, no matter what our background or personal circumstances. We humans are very good at judging both ourselves and others. If we level the playing field, we are more likely to see the Jesus in one another that is foundational to our faith. For Pope Francis, "Poverty is key, especially for consecrated life. It should be seen in everything. . . . [Poverty] begets spiritual life. That is, it engenders you, leading you to seek the only wealth that is what the Lord asks of you. It's the richness of discovering that one lives to serve."[5]

Theological Foundations: The Incarnation

Paul's letter to the Philippians emphasizes this humility we have as humans before God, beautifully calling out the great gift we receive in the person of Jesus, who "humbled himself" to become one of us, living as a human being out of love for all human beings. This is the greatest gift we receive from God, and yet the person of Jesus is only one gift

5. Francis, *Strength of Vocation*, 82–83.

among so many. The paradox in this humble recognition of our extreme poverty before God is that in knowing it, we also come to know our great richness. "Voluntary poverty, in the footsteps of Christ, is a symbol of Christ which is much esteemed, especially nowadays. Religious should cultivate it diligently and, if needs be, express it in new forms. It enables them to share in the poverty of Christ who for our sake became poor, though he was rich, so that we might become rich through his poverty" (*Perfectae Caritatis* 13). Paul's hymn of the incarnation is the foundation of theological meaning for poverty (Phil 2:5-11):

> Have among yourselves the same attitude that is also yours in Christ Jesus,
>
>> Who, though he was in the form of God,
>>> did not regard equality with God something to
>>>> be grasped.
>>> Rather, he emptied himself,
>>> taking the form of a slave,
>>> coming in human likeness;
>>> and found human in appearance,
>>> he humbled himself,
>>>> becoming obedient to death,
>>>> even death on a cross.
>> Because of this, God greatly exalted him
>>> and bestowed on him the name
>>> that is above every name,
>>> that at the name of Jesus
>>> every knee should bend,
>>> of those in heaven and on earth and under the earth,
>>> and every tongue confess that
>>> Jesus Christ is Lord,
>>> to the glory of God the Father.

The incarnation of God as Jesus Christ, a human who walked among us and lived as we do, lies at the core of the Christian faith. God, out of infinitely generous love for the human race, sent the Son to live on earth, to sanctify human life, and to save everyone from sin and death. The act of incarnation is the ultimate act of voluntary poverty. God became truly human, so that God's experience as a human being included all the vulnerability and pain as well as all the love and joy that each of us experiences in life. The almighty God, creator of all that exists, became a newborn child, completely dependent on his human mother for safety, nourishment, love, and care. His dependence models for us the dependence we have on God to care for us, provide for us daily. "This is the humiliation of Christ, his *kenosis*. But he does not take on the human sinful condition and its consequences to idealize it. It is rather because of the love for and solidarity with others who suffer it. It is to redeem them from their sin and to enrich them with his poverty. It is to struggle against human selfishness and everything that divides persons and allows that there be rich and poor, possessors and dispossessed, oppressors and oppressed."[6]

Paul reminds us that Jesus became as "slave," a term we must treat carefully today. Taken figuratively, the image of slavery reveals that God in choosing the incarnation became bound by the limitations of the human body, a far cry from the unlimited power and knowledge that God's essence contains and expresses. These limitations, chosen freely by God out of love, reveal the poverty of human existence: we are vulnerable, dependent on others (or one Other) for all we need, and we suffer hardships and pain. Though we might believe we need only rely on our ingenuity and intelligence, the contrast between God's all-powerful existence and the reality of baby Jesus in Mary's arms illustrates the vulnerability and reliance on others that is constituent of human existence. We, too, face the limitations of being human, the vulnerabilities of our physical, spiritual, mental, and emotional limitations.

6. Gutierrez, *Theology of Liberation*, 172.

We grow and learn new things, become older and forget, are wounded physically and emotionally. The poverty of human existence requires us to lean on one another's knowledge and abilities. It means we suffer and grieve over the vulnerabilities and wounds of those we love, just as Mary's heart was pierced by the suffering of her son. By choosing a vow of poverty, religious men and women acknowledge the vulnerability and dependence of being human, which then demands us to witness our humanity and share our gifts with those who are more vulnerable or who need us.

The poverty of being human is but one element illustrated in the incarnation. The family God chose as his human family was one of modest means, not poor in a way that denied them their human dignity, but poor in that their needs were met by daily work and reliance on one another. We can imagine them as relatively ordinary Jewish people of the time, not part of the ruling class or among those in power. Joseph, as an artisan, likely taught Jesus his craft and anticipated that he would take over his workshop. The house was probably multigenerational and filled with cousins and aunts and uncles.[7] While the men of the house took on work outside, the women probably worked together to provide the food for the daily table and to store food for months without harvest. Societal norms, unlike our individualistic notions, were focused on family life and social dependence.

Jesus's ministry and the early Christian communities seemed to place little value on monetary wealth. The first disciples came from all walks of life, including fishermen and wealthy women among them. The message preached by Jesus offered meaning, purpose, and joy, which all could identify with. The

7. Elizabeth A. Johnson's *Truly Our Sister: A Theology of Mary in the Communion of Saints* (London: Continuum, 2003) gives a lively and fulsome description of the social standards for Jewish families at the time. It is easy to imagine Mary's daily life through her research and descriptions.

earliest Christian communities, like the apostles, committed themselves to supporting one another. Paul's letters repeatedly admonish the early Christians to equality, reminding them that all they have is gift from God and no one can be placed over another in wealth or prestige because they did nothing to earn those gifts (e.g., 1 Cor 4). Obviously, Paul's admonition shows that equality was a struggle even so close to the time of Jesus. Paul reminds the early Christians that poverty and wealth are social realities that do not determine the worth of individuals and that we are called to help one another meet the physical needs of dignified human life. Social distinctions are not meant to divide, but rather to remind us that we all need one another.

The mystery of the incarnation of God in the vulnerable reality of being human is the theological exemplar of poverty. Jesus lived the poverty of God-become-human, subjected to the vulnerability and dependence inherent in human life. This wholehearted embrace of the human condition shows the generosity of God's love for the human race. Jesus's kenosis offers an example and provides meaning to the vow of poverty taken by religious today. The religious offers his or her whole self to God, in recognition of God's infinite love and the complete dependence of being human. This theological basis, then, forms the foundation for the response to the poverty of the world today.

Jesus proclaimed a gospel message that attracted people of all sorts to him and to the Christian path. Central to all human beings is the need to make meaning of life, the desire to know our purpose and to find joy. The call of voluntary poverty recognizes that financial resources can never provide this meaning and joy. At the same time it calls us to solidarity with those who do not have the basic necessities that support human dignity. The constant presence of poor people and communities among us, always at the periphery of power and prestige, draws the attention and care of women and men religious as another place that needs the preaching of the kingdom of God and action to bring that kingdom into reality.

The Call of Poverty in Today's World

The rapidity of communication in today's world draws our awareness to realities previously unrecognized. We must open our eyes to the needs not only of our neighborhood but of the whole world. This awareness extends as well to our ability to see and therefore change the effect our actions have on the world around us. Poverty is at the center of most of the problems in our world today. The World Bank notes that for twenty years, until the setbacks of the global pandemic, global poverty was in decline. It is estimated that between 703 and 729 million people live in extreme poverty at the end of 2020, defined as less than $1.90 per day; 24.1 percent of the world's population live on less than $3.20/day, and 43.6 percent on less than $5.50/day.[8] These numbers paint a dire picture for nearly half of the world. In the United States and other Western nations, we relegate the consequences of our overconsumption to places that are hidden from us and far from our own backyards. We can no longer claim that our use of the world's resources does not cause chaos or damage in other parts of the world. As religious, we must open our eyes to witness the effects of what we do and most especially the effects on those who have fewer resources.

Women religious especially have been at the forefront of recognizing the emergency situation of our earth, whether from the pipeline project (fought by the Adorers of the Blood of

8. The World Bank keeps extensive data on poverty in the world and projects poverty rates into the future. See https://www.worldbank.org/en /topic/poverty, accessed May 20, 2021.

Christ) or by deforestation in the Amazon rainforest, for which Sr. Dorothy Stang, SNDdeN, died. Commitment to good stewardship of the world's resources is both for the sake of those who are poor, as they are disproportionately affected by Western materialism, and for the sake of the planet and everything that lives on it. We recognize in the world God's creation and its blessedness. In Genesis, we learn that God created all that exists. When God created human beings, they were intended to be co-creators with God, responsible for care of the planet. While at one time theologians taught that humans have "dominion over creation," today we recognize the damage done by the mentality that dominion meant forcing the planet to meet our needs. Instead, today's theologians focus on the need to care for the planet. We see that our reliance on the gifts of the earth has been excessive and destructive. Pope Francis states in *Evangelii Gaudium,* "With due respect for the autonomy and culture of every nation, we must never forget that the planet belongs to all mankind and is meant for all mankind; the mere fact that some people are born in places with fewer resources or less development does not justify that they are living with less dignity" (190). The fragility of our ecosystem and the unjust burden it places on vulnerable populations calls to us in ways we have never before in history known.

As women and men religious, we are uniquely able to call attention to these issues. We are linked to others by vocation, and our connections around the world bring home the devastating realities of human-caused and natural disasters. From our place at the peripheries, we offer our witness to those in power. Our call is not only to help those individuals we find in need, but also to work to change social structures. By membership in communities and through intercongregational work, we can become a powerful force to prophecy among the powerful in our world.

Pope Francis often speaks of the joy that we can learn through getting to know people who are poor. "The poor person, when loved, 'is esteemed as of great value,' and this is what makes the authentic option for the poor differ from any other ideology, from any attempt to exploit the poor for one's own personal or political interest. Only on the basis of this real and sincere closeness can we properly accompany the poor on their path of liberation" (*Evangelii Gaudium* 199). Today, more than ever, we are needed on the peripheries. Through solidarity with others, we as Christians in general and religious in particular offer a way of living in community and communion with people who are very different from ourselves. Sometimes that means living a life of simplicity and community in a motherhouse surrounded by wealthy neighborhoods. More often, it means adapting to the lifestyle of those who surround us, when we find ourselves in neighborhoods with lesser means. Always, it means demonstrating to the world through our lives that it is possible to live in a way that uses less, sharing our lives with diverse populations, helping others as we see there is need.

Finally, the world today needs voices who assert the futility of material possessions. We are inundated with advertisements that tell us what products will make us happier or more fulfilled, and experimentation with those products quickly leads us to the knowledge that those things cannot bring joy. Vowing to live in simple poverty helps us to see that only by breaking out of the cycle of purchasing things for happiness can we find true joy and fulfillment. The more we can witness in the world that simplicity brings us joy, the more impact we can have on the joy of those around us.

In addition to the material poverty that exists in the world, poverty can be found in other dimensions, even among those who are materially wealthy. The CICLSAL document "Starting Afresh from Christ" brings these realities to life:

> Despair at the lack of meaning in life, drug addiction, fear of abandonment in old age or sickness, marginalization

or social discrimination are new forms of poverty which have been added to its traditional forms. Mission, in its traditional and new forms, is first of all a service to the dignity of the person in a dehumanized society because the greatest and most serious poverty of our time is the callous treading upon the rights of the human person. With the dynamism of charity, of forgiveness, and of reconciliation, consecrated persons strive in justice to build a world which offers new and better possibilities for the life and development of the individual.[9]

In short, religious men and women find ministries that strive to alleviate any and all poverties that prevent any human person from living out the fullness of his or her life.

A Spirituality of Poverty, Not a Spiritual Poverty

There are two ways to connect poverty and spirituality. The first is a sort of spiritual poverty: I recognize my limitations and know that I am nothing in comparison to the blessings I have received from God. This type of poverty might include the deprivations that I have suffered in my life, the times I have felt incapable of accomplishing something or faced the boundaries of my ability. This is, yes, one way of approaching poverty's connection to my spirituality. It is a helpful way to recognize my own abilities and to experience a solidarity with others who have similar needs.

A deeper spirituality of poverty arises when we are able to recognize the gift that God abundantly gives us. This spiritu-

9. CICLSAL, "Starting Afresh from Christ: A Renewed Commitment to Consecrated Life in the Third Millennium" (Vatican City: Libreria Editrice Vaticana, 2002), 13, https://www.vatican.va/roman_curia/congregations /ccscrlife/documents/rc_con_ccscrlife_doc_20020614_ripartire-da-cristo _en.html, 35.

ality of poverty begins with gratitude.[10] In knowing we have everything out of God's great abundance and by God's great love for us, we are inspired to give thanks for what we have received. Gratitude is only possible when we do not believe we have earned it for ourselves, but when we know deep within that our lives are all gift. Giving thanks for the gifts God freely showers on us opens our hearts to a deep sense of joy that comes from knowing we are incredibly loved by God. Even a small taste of that unwavering love, glimpsed in the tiniest of flashes, brings a joy that is mysterious in its greatness.

The natural outcomes of gratitude are stewardship and generosity. God's creation, which we were given use of for life, needs our careful stewardship. Fostering growth and health of the earth enables it to continue to support life for our lifetimes and that of generations to come. Our duty to the earth that provides so generously to us is simply to care for it in response. Secondly, gratitude for all I have received is repaid with generosity toward others. If nothing is really mine, then I can freely give of myself without counting the cost. This is an act of self-emptying, echoing the kerygma of Christ on the cross. Just as he gave all for us, so too I am called to give of what I have to those who have need. Our faith helps us remember that what we need will be given to us, and in charity we seek to provide generously for the needs of others.

The recent pandemic has helped us as a human population realize what we hold dear and how we prioritize the things we value. We are learning that a simpler life, with less "busy" and more time at home, can be fulfilling. We miss our families and

10. See the work of David Steindl-Rast, including his book *Gratefulness, the Heart of Prayer: An Approach to Life in Fullness* (New York: Paulist Press, 1984) and his June 2013 TEDGlobal talk, "Want to Be Happy? Be Grateful," https://www.ted.com/talks/david_steindl_rast_want_to_be _happy_be_grateful?language=en.

friends, and we are learning to rely on one another for support in different ways than we could have imagined before. Most importantly, perhaps, the higher rates of suffering and death have brought into clearer focus the precious value of human life and relationships with those we love. We are all too aware, in this age of instant communication, that every community around the world is suffering with the same illness. We share in the suffering of the world, and the inequities of the world are highlighted by the disease's progression and deadliness. Our eyes have been opened, and I hope that our priorities and practices will be revised as we emerge from this dark time.

Eschatological Vision

The call to solidarity with the poor brings us to the peripheries, to work toward radical inclusion of everyone in this life as a prefigure of the next, the fullness of life in God.

Pope Francis constantly calls Christians to be among those who are at the peripheries. When we go to the edges of society, we do not leave behind the talents, privileges, and power that we have. Instead, we are called to use what we have for the benefit of others. The goal of going out to the margins, to the edges or peripheries, is never to simply be there: we go out to those who are marginalized in order to bring them into greater inclusion in society. Power and privilege are assets that do not define who we are, and so we do not hold onto them too tightly. Rather, the privilege and power we have as religious allows us to re-create, re-center structures in favor, always, of human dignity for everyone. We have seen in recent decades that the rich people of the world are getting richer while those who do not have enough is an increasing population, with a widening gap of wealth between the two sides. Increasing one's own bank account while depriving others of basic needs does not bring human fulfillment on either side.

Jesus's vision demonstrates that there is another way of being that is open to us, one that brings meaning and joy to those who seek it. As consecrated men and women, we recognize that Jesus's vision must dominate our worldview, giving meaning to our mission and allowing us to share joy with others. Poverty might be the most concrete area for prophetic witness: removing wealth from our equation of human dignity turns societal norms on their head. Our witness to voluntary poverty as a way of life and a way of solidarity with others can then prefigure the kingdom of God promised by Jesus.

Conclusion

This chapter has focused primarily on the issue of material poverty, particularly that which is voluntarily chosen by consecrated religious as a way of devoting their lives wholeheartedly to God. Spiritual poverty is a reality that religious are called to respond to as well. As one author puts it, calling it "intellectual poverty," "To take away people's hope, to tell them that nothing is going to change, that nothing will get better, is to deny the gift of prophecy in the life of the Church. Prophets are about spreading hope, giving people a vision of where we are going, of what we are called to be. Intellectual poverty is the inability to even imagine a better society, to be incapable of aspiring to a future that is not simply a repetition of the past."[11]

By their vow of poverty, consecrated religious commit themselves to challenge the reality of the poverties of our world, to live simply in order to use the earth's resources more responsibly, and to stand in solidarity with those who

11. Kenneth R. Himes, "Poverty and Christian Discipleship," in *Poverty: Responding Like Jesus*, ed. Kenneth R. Himes and Conor M. Kelly (Brewster, MA: Paraclete Press, 2018), 17.

are genuinely poor by witnessing to the injustice and inhumanity of material poverty. Living simply and advocating for human dignity prefigures the glory of the kingdom of God, the joy and fulfillment for which human beings were created.

In religious communities, poverty is lived out together, so that religious challenge each other and the wider culture to greater simplicity and a lighter footprint on the earth. Religious discern together to determine the use of resources, focusing on imitation of Jesus and his simplicity, acknowledging the needs and ministry of the congregation. Each one striving to follow Christ according to the community's charism, poverty is lived out in many different ways by different congregations. Yet for each one, the vow of voluntary poverty challenges society's norms and places the religious in solidarity with those on the margins.

CHAPTER FIVE

The Vow of Celibacy

Introduction

As we saw in the first chapter, one of the foundational characteristics of human beings, given by God at creation, is the need for companionship and community. According to Genesis 2, woman was created to accompany man in life. Our need for others is ingrained in the very depths of our being. While for most people, this means marriage and family, for religious it means a commitment of a different sort. The vow of chastity or celibacy expresses our commitment to others as one of community and availability, marked by a radical openness to human connection that can be expressed in generosity to all.

"Chastity" refers to the practice of refraining from sexual activity outside of a committed relationship. "Celibacy" refers to abstaining from *all* sexual activity. Religious vows, according to canon law, use the terminology of a vow of chastity. Yet, celibacy more accurately describes the practice of the vow itself in the context of religious life. The vow of chastity commits the religious woman or man to a life abstaining from physical expressions of sexuality of any kind.

Celibacy and chastity are concepts that have multiple levels of meaning, however, and living as a healthy celibate means grappling with the different layers that comprise our human sexuality. Beyond technically following the rules, what behaviors and thought patterns prevent me from living out the fullness of my being? Any obsessive thought or behavior, whether tied to my sexuality or not, can pull me away from contributing my gifts to the world around me, in the way God envisioned for my life. Additionally, how we view our bodies and our desires can affect our mental health and our ability to relate to anyone, including God. Acknowledging and understanding ourselves as God's beloved creatures and experiencing the joy of all that we are leads us to deeper relationships and greater confidence in how we share our gifts with others.

Definitions of chastity that focus on what behavior it avoids are rarely a helpful guide to life. Religious understand this vow in different ways, and all must find a fulfilling lifestyle that includes the vow. Like the marriage vow, the vow of chastity binds the individual in a relationship. This relationship is with God, lived out in the expressed celibate love we have for those around us. In this chapter, we will discuss the vow of chastity as a window opening space within us to focus our lives on love, community, and the freedom to share our gifts with others.

This chapter focuses on the vow of celibacy in several aspects. Celibacy challenges both the societal norms regarding sexuality and the church's history of denying any goodness to sexuality beyond procreation. In seeking out a more holistic view of the vow of celibacy, this chapter will focus on several areas: celibacy as a reflection of Jesus's command to love one another, celibacy as commitment to community life through the image of community given to us by the Trinity, and the vow of celibacy as a commitment that brings freedom and honors fidelity. The chapter concludes by addressing some of the contemporary issues facing religious communities today, including the need for a more compassionate view of the human body and a reckoning with the past relegation of sexuality to conversations about sinfulness alone.

Historical Views of Celibacy

All of the early monastic communities saw the need for the support of communal living, just as the group that Jesus gathered around himself did. They prayed together, shared their material goods, and embraced asceticism. Their asceticism normally included a simple diet, celibacy, and extended periods of prayer. Most of the earliest monastics were not focused on penitence, as would later be more common. The image of their lives was one of joy and simplicity, care for one another, and close relationship with God. St. Benedict calls their life in common "a school of the Lord's service," emphasizing the continual growth to which each monk is called (RB Prol. 45).

The monastic movement in early Christianity included the practice of virginity or celibacy. Early in the teaching of the church, virginity or chastity became marks of holiness, showing a devotedness to the Christian practice running counter to societal expectations and norms. The theology that supported these practices and explained them for the believing community reflected a dualistic worldview. Dualism predates Christianity, and it was held by Jewish and Christian communities in the early Common Era, as well as non-religious philosophical systems. Dualism taught that the world is of basically two parts, one light and good, and one dark and evil. The material realm and all that it contains is part of the dark side of existence, while the spiritual realities are part of the good and light. The human person, then, contains both: the soul and spiritual world are holy and light, while all that is physical, including physical needs and desires, forms part of the dark side, part of what is not holy in us. As this dualistic worldview became dominant in Christianity, the material realm became contrasted to the divine spiritual realm. Natural human processes, including human needs such as food and sleep as well as our sexuality, became equated with the negative. Those striving for holiness developed ascetical practices that reflected this worldview, and fasting, prayer vigils, and chastity became identifying characteristics of sanctity. Self-denial is a way that helps us seek God, but dualism when it shapes our understanding of the human person can lead to destruction. As time went on, and bodies were valued as even less holy, the woman's body in particular became equated with something evil. As many theologians have pointed out, the woman's body is carnal: out of woman comes children, and the generative process connects women's bodies to physical reality in a messy physical way. Additionally, these processes were largely mysterious to the men who wrote theology. By declaring their own natural God-given desires for companionship as evil, men were led to believe that women were evil as well.

Today, a healthy spirituality must include balance between the physical and spiritual, recognizing that God created us with both. Creation and the incarnation bless the physical no less than the spiritual. Women and men are both good in their createdness, in their bodies and their souls. Sexuality, as one part of a holistic view of the human person, must reclaim its place in our conversations on Christianity, religious life, and even sanctity.

Love and Community

The vow of chastity is about our human call to love. This vow directs the lives of religious to follow Jesus as the guide to relationships and relationality with others. Central to the message of Jesus is the command to love one another. Every path to which Christians are called holds this imperative as foundational. While the word "love" is used in many different ways today, Jesus's directives are clear: care for others, honor the humanity of each person, and help each one you encounter to live as whole a life as possible.

The actions and words of Jesus show the importance of caring for one another. In the parable of the Good Samaritan (Luke 10:25-37), one of the main points is that one's goodness comes from how one treats a stranger, particularly when one's actions will not receive recognition. The Samaritan sees a stranger in need and acts to help him. Others, even those who have a reputation for being good people, see the one in need and walk past, even crossing the road to avoid him. No one is watching them, and the Samaritan stops without needing recognition for what he's done. In addition, he provides for future needs and promises to stop again on his way back. Like the Samaritan, Jesus takes the time to meet the physical needs of others, witnessed to in the many stories of healing that the gospels recount. One among multitudes is the man born blind. Jesus stops and spends time with him, spitting into the dirt to make mud and anointing the man twice before his vision clears. He heals his physical need, making time to attend to the person before him.

Physical need is only part of the human experience. Jesus illustrates many times the need for emotional or spiritual healing as well. The hemorrhaging woman (Mark 5:25-34) provides one example: while she reaches for Jesus's cloak to touch it and be healed, he stops to speak to her, helping her recognize the importance of her faith and her return to participation in society. Another, the woman who washes his feet with her tears (Luke 7:36-60), is embraced as a model of hospitality in a household that wouldn't recognize her presence. A striking witness to the connection of body and spiritual care occurs when the paralytic is healed, as Jesus says "your sins are forgiven" (Mark 2:1-12).

Through the witness of the gospels, we see that healing is both on the outside and on the inside—physical, emotional, and spiritual. This is the model of love Jesus offers his followers: we must bear witness to the humanity of one another, to the dignity of the human person, no matter who that person is and what he or she might have done in life.

"Love one another as I have loved you" (see John 13:34): as Jesus honors the dignity of every human person, so too we are called to uphold human dignity.

Jesus's love led him to the cross, to lay down his life for those he loves, which includes everyone. Even today, Christians follow him in laying down their lives for others. Mother Teresa is a poignant example of a life given completely to uphold human dignity.[1] She offered her whole self to care for others in the most extreme circumstances. Every gift, talent, morsel of energy, and waking hour was spent in service to those most in need of her love. We are all called to be saints: how do I use my talents, energy, and call to serve those around me? An honest answer reveals my love for others.

The Trinity: Prototype for Human Community

Theological anthropology illustrates our need for human companionship. How we live together in community is a reflection of the very nature of God whose image and likeness we bear. The Christian teaching on the Trinity is the great mystery of our faith: God, we believe, is one God, and God is also three. The paradox of this teaching must be understood by a bit of a philosophical dance. The only way it makes any sense to us is to remember that the boundaries of humanity are not the same as those of divinity. That means that though a human being can only be one person, the divine Being can be three Persons. While singular in divinity, God is also communal in identity. The Catholic faith embraces this mystery without explaining it away. The Trinity will always be beyond what we can understand or express with human language,

---

1. See Mother Teresa's posthumously published letters and journals, *Come Be My Light*, ed. Brian Kolodiejchuk (New York: Crown Publishing, 2007).

and we will continue to use our language and intellect to explore this great mystery. Reflecting on our human nature, we see hints of the divine mystery within, beyond our words and understanding. Because human beings are made in the image and likeness of God, that image and likeness must include God's trinitarian nature in some way. One way to understand how we reflect God's Trinity is through the community.

Human beings are social creatures. We are meant to live in communities. Innate within us is the desire to be with others. On the level of nature, this leads us to partners, sex, and children. Less carnal desires lead us to seek intimacy through deep conversations and close friendships. We long for people to spend time with, to talk to, to eat with, to live with, and on and on, as we learned throughout the isolation of the global pandemic. Primal human instincts led the earliest human communities to remain together in groups. Like other animals, we find strength in numbers. Alone, a human being is vulnerable to the dangers of the world. In communities, we have greater strength and security for survival. When we add our rational capacities, this communal tendency multiplies the security we find when we are together.

Theologically, the need for community is reflected in our communal relationship with God. God made a covenant with our Jewish ancestors as a people, not as individuals. Early in his papacy, Francis explained the theological significance of belonging to a group: "In the history of salvation, God has saved a people. There is no full identity without belonging to a people. No one is saved alone, as an isolated individual, but God attracts us looking at the complex web of relationships that take place in the human community. God enters into this dynamic, this participation in the web of human relationships."[2]

---

2. Pope Francis, in an interview with Antonio Spadaro, "A Big Heart Open to God," *America* September 30, 2013, https://www.americamagazine.org/faith/2013/09/30/big-heart-open-god-interview-pope-francis.

Our lives echo the divine Trinity in how we relate to one another. The mystery of the Trinity allows for union and diversity. The three persons of the Trinity are indivisible—they must remain in community. And yet they are distinct, particularly as we understand their relationship with human beings. The Father is Creator, relating to us analogously to a human father, providing for our needs and not only creating us at the beginning of our lives but continuing to create us throughout all our lifespan. The Son, whom we call Redeemer, relates to us more as a brother, teacher, and companion, who literally gave up his life for us so that we can be united with him for eternity. The Holy Spirit relates to us in yet a different way, indwelling in each of us and uniting us as church, inspiring us to use the gifts we have been given, and motivating us to follow the path of Jesus. Through the Holy Spirit we come to recognize the great diversity of the human population, and the necessity of diversity within each community, in order to meet the many needs of human beings. Thus, the three of the Trinity models for us the importance of union in a community in such a way that all the diversity is honored and held together. This doctrine, then, can be for us an inspiration for community living.

Beyond a recognition and coexistence of different people with varied and diverse gifts, human community must model the functional collaboration of the divine Trinity. The Father never acts alone—nor does the Son or the Spirit. In every moment, in every action, the three act as one. A united human community multiplies the potential of the individual members. The whole is indeed greater than the sum of its parts. God's infinite creativity and generativity is shared by us when we unite with one another to work towards the kingdom of God, the Beloved Community.

The Trinity might be imagined as a ball of fire in perpetual motion, constantly fed by the energy of love between the three Persons. Our own human sexual energy is also generative and creative, and our use of that energy reflects the power of the

Holy Spirit. Like God's unbridled creation, we too must use our energy in ways that bring life and newness into the world. The impulse to have children exists in religious, even though they do not become parents. Instead, that life-giving energy must be directed outward in relationship, to help others grow into themselves and to let them know they are loved. The creative generative energy never ceases. If we, in our human communities, could only touch the love of the Trinity, the effects of our actions would be greater than we could imagine.

Freedom through Commitment

Human beings offer love to others in many different ways, and the most profound offerings of love include commitment to one another. For most, this commitment involves marriage between two people, a commitment which extends to children and other family. In religious life, vows commit one's life to God. Christians are not the first or the only people to make vows to God, and predecessors are found in the Old Testament. The concept of "covenant," which illustrates for us the fidelity of God to God's people, offers a starting point to understand the strength of this bond. In the Old Testament, God and the people of Israel form covenants in which the people promise to follow God's law and God promises to remain with them. Invariably, the people fail to uphold their end of the covenant, and God continues to be with them. Fidelity of one to the other marks the people as chosen, as God's people, as a nation beloved in a special way. Though the people are overcome by fear again and again, God continues to provide guidance, protection, and nourishment even as they experience hardships. God is faithful to human beings, in accord with God's identity, and forgiving of our human faults.

Though the Israelites struggle to trust God's fidelity, their covenant with God remains strong and true. In that context, the people find a new sort of freedom. By trusting God and following Moses, they literally are taken from slavery and into new life. God guides them through the desert, protects them from their pursuers, and provides food and water to nourish their bodies. Moses and Aaron, acting together as mediators with God, reassure the people of God's fidelity and present them with the Ten Commandments.

Here we find a paradox: God and the people form a covenant, one that binds them forever to each other. And yet, in this binding, this commitment, they are freed from slavery in Egypt. Commitment today both binds and frees us. Choosing to commit to one way of life allows that life to flourish and expand in ways that are unimaginable before commitment. While it may seem counterintuitive, a life lacking commitment does not allow the depth of living that commitment allows. Covenant promises that whatever we seek, we are not alone. Commitment assures us that we are rooted and grounded in love and life with one another, which allows us to take risks and live knowing that there is a safety net, a community waiting to catch us if we fall. Together, united, we are stronger and able to live more vibrantly than each one alone.

Another element to commitment is the knowledge that I cannot do this alone. The first sin of Adam and Eve showed our human tendency to deny our limitations and distrust what we have been told. They sought knowledge that was reserved for God alone, reaching beyond their capacity because they did not believe God's word. Commitment and fidelity help us to recognize our human limitations and know that we cannot live without others and without God. By committing myself to the vows, I am saying that I put my talents and gifts at the feet of others, and I entrust myself to their care as well. This is a form of humility: I know who I am and what I have to offer, and I also know who I am not and how much I must rely on others, most especially on God's freely offered love and gift.

Catherine of Siena receives a message from God in her visions that illustrates the importance of recognizing our gifts and the gifts of others:

> In this mortal life, so long as you are pilgrims, I have bound you with the chain of charity. Whether you want it or not, you are so bound. If you should break loose by not wanting to live in charity for your neighbors, you will still be bound by it by force. Thus, that you may practice charity in action and in will, I in my providence did not give to any one person or to each individually the knowledge for doing everything necessary for human life.
>
> No, I gave something to one, something else to another, so that each one's need would be a reason to have recourse to the other. . . .
>
> Could I not have given everyone everything? Of course. But in my providence, I wanted to make each of you dependent on the others, so that you would be forced to exercise charity in action and will at once. I have shown you my generosity, goodness, and providence toward people.[3]

Eschatological Dimensions of the Vow of Celibacy

Like the other vows, celibacy provides a powerful critique of society. In addition to revealing the inability of physical pleasure to bring lasting happiness, celibacy reminds us of Paul's statement that in the life to come, marriage will be no more. Our interpersonal relationships are re-ordered so that no single relationship is placed above the others. By choosing not to have children and a nuclear family, those in

---

3. Catherine of Siena, *The Dialogues*, trans. Suzanne Noffke (New York: Paulist, 1980), 148.

consecrated life place their hope in God's promise of a future of justice and peace. In this light, celibacy is not simply a practical choice to allow for a greater commitment to mission, but it is also a theological choice to witness to a future we can only imagine.

It is important to dwell on the social critique offered by the vow of celibacy. So much of modern culture is shaped by messages of sexuality, desire, and pleasure. It is in advertisements (even for products that have nothing to do with sex), in fashion and art, in the looks-obsessed diet industry, and in music and movies. All of these areas send the message that we will be happy if only we have enough sex or the perfect partner. A vow of celibacy, within the context of a holistic religious life, pushes back on these messages with the faith in fulfillment that is found not in pleasure but in relationships, wholeness, mission, and ultimately God's unfailing love for us.

Conclusion

This discussion on the vow of celibacy focused on relationships, the ability for one who has vowed to a celibate life to form deep and lasting connections with others because of his or her free commitment to Jesus. The freedom opened up by this commitment is exemplified in the community of persons that is the reality of the Trinity, which human beings share in by virtue of being made in God's image and likeness. Living in local communities, connected to the congregation as a whole by charism and relationship, religious express the total gift of self to God through their love and union with others. Their joy challenges society's messages that our fulfillment should come from pleasure and superficial relationships over the lasting happiness that building a life in God brings.

Despite the joy of celibate life, the church still has many issues in the area of sexuality that need attention. Most fundamentally, ignoring human development in the area of sexuality for religious and priests leads to secrecy and immaturity, which certainly have contributed to the profoundly disturbing sex abuse scandal in the church. A better formation, one which does not ignore or deny realities about human desires, including homosexuality and gender diversity, is needed among all religious.

Theology, too, must be cautious not to fall into either ignoring human sexuality or relegating the physical body to a secondary status below all things that are spiritual. God's creation is both material and spiritual, and so we must consider both as good things created by God. Recognizing that the dualistic viewpoint is no longer viable will help reduce the tendency to place men (long considered predominantly spiritual beings) over women (whose physicality through procreation cannot be denied). A more realistic view on creation removes this dualism and at the same time eliminates binary distinctions from the vocabulary. Greater nuance will lead to healthier theology.

Conclusion

Exploring the relationship between consecrated life and theology has allowed us to see how religious life, today and always, points in the direction of God's dream for all creation. The image of God in which we were created lies in our call to follow God's will, using our creativity and freedom to imagine a world in which no one is suffering. While all Christians are called to this reality, consecrated religious live it out in a more intentional way, committed to a deep relationship with God that removes other obligations and allows this focus to be primary. Religious men and women imitate Christ through poverty, chastity, and obedience, calling out the false happiness and ultimate dissatisfaction that seeking wealth, false love, and power lead to. Instead, a life of voluntary poverty acknowledges that all good things come from God and we are dependent on God and one another for everything. A commitment to celibacy allows religious to share their love for people far and wide, echoing the universal unconditional love of God for each individual. The vow of obedience acknowledges the freedom of committing one's life to God's path, choosing discernment as a daily lifelong task. The three vows together form the center of religious life, one in which these elements are integrated for fullness of human existence and prophetic witness to the hope and joy of the Christian faith.

As prophetic witnesses to an eschatological reality, religious profess three vows that challenge the world as it is with a vision of a world that is better, more aligned with God's desires for it. Obedience calls into account those who wield power for their own benefit at the expense of others. Discernment and freedom in their purest forms lead humans to follow the call of God for their lives, which must work for the good of all over the good of one. Freedom is only free when it works toward what is good. Poverty challenges the world's inequitable distribution of wealth, which excludes a majority of people from fullness of life and a healthy participation in the world economy. It also demonstrates that the amassing of wealth is not a true way to a meaningful life and the joy that God wishes for us. Celibacy challenges societal messages about sexuality and physical desire, calling us to wider community with others and turning away from independence that isolates. In addition, not seeking out children and family points to a larger family in the human race, and that our future in the world to come does not require progeny in this world. Meaning in life is found in our love for one another, a love that wants the best for each one and for the community as a whole.

Prophetic witness involves, first, the critique of culture as it is, drawing attention through challenge or grief to the elements of society that deny the dignity of the human person. The very presence of religious committed to obedience, poverty, and celibacy embodies this societal critique. The second piece of prophetic witness involves imagining a world that is different. Christians believe in a world in which all have their needs met and live the fullness of life that God wants for them. We envision this world on earth now; after all, Jesus preached that "the kingdom of God is at hand!" We also envision this world as the heavenly banquet to which God calls his beloved people. Religious men and women live "in the meantime," between the world as it is now and the world to come. In the here and now, the ministries of religious strive to make progress toward the end of oppression, violence, and need on earth. In the presence and commitment of religious, the witness of another way of being offers the joy and hope for a future that is better than the present. "In order to truly live in the image and likeness of God, our being and doing ought to be intrinsically interrelated."[1] The hope to which religious witness is union with Jesus, a return to our source and complete fulfillment of the dream of God for each of us. Thus, the joy of religious life is a witness to the hope for wholeness, meaning, and, ultimately, the joy of eternal life in Love, in God.

Religious life is a constant throughout the history of the church, but only because it has been able to address both needs that are universal and those that are timely. As religious life moves into the future, how do we hold onto the prophetic witness of joy that we offer? What things must we let go of to continue to speak to the world as it is now? What questions must we ask; what ministries must we embrace? How will we continue to point to a better world, to heaven? How will we continue to be prophetic witnesses of joy in our world?

---

1. Martin Poulsom, "Sustaining Presence: Religious Life in the Midst of Creation," in *A Future Full of Hope?*, ed. Gemma Simmonds (Collegeville, MN: Liturgical Press, 2012), 57.

Selected Bibliography

Ambrosio, Márian. "Weaving Solidarity for Life: Living and Witnessing as Women Religious of Apostolic Life." Keynote Address presented at the International Union of Superiors General Plenary Assembly, Rome, May 9–13, 2016. http://www.international unionsuperiorsgeneral.org/wp-content/uploads/2016/04/Pl-2016 _Marian-Ambrosio_ENG.pdf.

Arbuckle, Gerald A. "Suffocating Religious Life: A New Type Emerges." *The Way* 65 (1989). http://www.theway.org.uk/Back /s065Arbuckle.pdf.

Arnaiz, José M. "The Great Challenges of Consecrated Life Today." Capitolo General FSP, 2013. http://archive.paoline.org/paoline /allegati/15808/Arnaiz_LegrandiSfideVCoggi-eng.pdf.

Brueggemann, Walter. *The Prophetic Imagination*. 2nd ed. Minneapolis: Fortress, 2001.

Byrne, Brendan. "A Future for Religious Life?" *The Furrow* 68, no. 2 (February 2017): 94–103.

Chittister, Joan. *The Fire in These Ashes: A Spirituality of Contemporary Religious Life*. Kansas City, MO: Sheed and Ward, 1995.

Cimperman, Maria. *Religious Life for Our World: Creating Communities of Hope*. Maryknoll, NY: Orbis, 2020.

Cole, Donna. "In the Company of Saints: Participating in Religious Life." *Ministry & Liturgy* 40, no. 7 (September 2013): 19.

Collins, Julie. "Celibate Love as Contemplation." *Review for Religious* January–February 2000: 79–86.

Congregation for Institutes of Consecrated Life and Societies of Apostolic Life (CICLSAL). "*Faciem tuam, Domine, requiram*: The Service of Authority and Obedience." Vatican City: Libreria Editrice Vaticana, 2008. http://www.vatican.va/roman

_curia/congregations/ccscrlife/documents/rc_con_ccscrlife_doc
_20080511_autorita-obbedienza_en.html.

CICLSAL. "Keep Watch! To Consecrated Men and Women Journeying in the Footsteps of God." Vatican City: Libreria Editrice
Vaticana, 2014.

CICLSAL. "Rejoice! A Letter to Consecrated Men and Women: A
Message from the Teachings of Pope Francis," Vatican City: Libreria Editrice Vaticana, 2014, 52. http://www.vatican.va/roman
_curia/congregations/ccscrlife/documents/rc_con_ccscrlife_doc
_20140202_rallegratevi-lettera-consacrati_en.pdf.

CICLSAL. "Starting Afresh from Christ: A Renewed Commitment
to Consecrated Life in the Third Millennium." Vatican City:
Libreria Editrice Vaticana, 2002. https://www.vatican.va/roman
_curia/congregations/ccscrlife/documents/rc_con_ccscrlife
_doc_20020614_ripartire-da-cristo_en.html.

Council of Major Superiors of Women Religious, eds. *The Foundations of Religious Life: Revisiting the Vision.* Notre Dame, IN:
Ave Maria Press, 2009.

Crosby, Michael. *Can Religious Life Be Prophetic?* New York:
Crossroad, 2004.

Cummings, Kathleen Sprows. *Understanding U.S. Catholic Sisters
Today.* Washington, DC: FADICA, 2015. http://www.national
catholicsistersweek.org/_resources/FDC_001_Report.pdf.

Downey, Paula. "Religious Life for a World of Transition." *The
Furrow* 60, no. 11 (November 2009): 612–20.

Dunn, Ted. "Refounding Religious Life: A Choice for Transforma-
tional Change." *Human Development* 30, no. 3 (2009): 5–13.

Fiand, Barbara. *Refocusing the Vision: Religious Life into the Future.* New York: Crossroads, 2001.

Flood, David. "Poverty and the Gospel." *Franciscan Studies* 64
(2006): 1–15.

Francis. "Address of the Holy Father." September 27, 2015. http://
w2.vatican.va/content/francesco/en/speeches/2015/september
/documents/papa-francesco_20150927_usa-detenuti.html.

Francis. "Apostolic Letter to All Consecrated People on the Occasion
of the Year of Consecrated Life," November 21, 2014. https://
w2.vatican.va/content/francesco/en/apost_letters/documents
/papa-francesco_lettera-ap_20141121_lettera-consacrati.html.

Francis. *Fratelli Tutti: Encyclical Letter on Fraternity and Social Friendship.* Vatican City: Libreria Editrice Vaticana, 2020.

Francis. *Gaudete et Exsultate: Apostolic Exhortation on the Call to Holiness in Today's World.* Vatican City: Libreria Editrice Vaticana, 2018. https://www.vatican.va/content/francesco/en /apost_exhortations/documents/papa-francesco_esortazione -ap_20180319_gaudete-et-exsultate.html.

Francis. "Homily for the Presentation of the Lord and XXI World Day of Consecrated Life." February 2, 2017. https://w2.vatican.va /content/francesco/en/homilies/2017/documents/papa-francesco _20170202_omelia-vita-consacrata.html.

Francis. *The Strength of Vocation: Consecrated Life Today, a Conversation with Fernando Prado.* Quezon City, Philippines: Claretian Publications, 2018.

Gallares, Judette A. "Testimony of the Faithful on Consecrated Life." *Landas* 30, no. 1 (2016): 51–56.

Garcia, Elise, Daniel Horan, and Tracy Kemme. "Poverty: New Thoughts on an Old Vow." *Horizon* 42, no. 2 (2017): 5–13.

Goergen, Donald. "Religious Life and the Gospel." In *Letters to My Brothers and Sisters.* Dublin, Ireland: Dominican Publications, 1996.

Gray, Howard. "Freedom and Discernment: A Life-Long Pilgrimage." *Human Development* 37 (Summer 2017): 6–15.

Gray, Howard. "Exploring Three Dimensions of the Vow of Obedience." *Horizon* 28, no. 3 (Fall 2003): 7–10.

Guinan, Michael D. "Religious Poverty: Witness to the Risen Christ." *Horizon* 28, no. 2 (Summer 2003): 17–20.

Hahnenberg, Edward P. "Theology of Vocation: Attuned to the Voice of God." *Human Development* 36, no. 3 (Spring 2016): 54–59.

Harrison, Ben. "Eros and the Call to Religious Life." *Human Development* 33, no. 2 (Summer 2012): 34–39.

Harrison, Ben. "Perseverance Just for Today." *Human Development* 31, no. 3 (Fall 2010).

Haughey, John C. "Freedom and Commitment." *The Way* 15, no. 2 (April 1975): 111–18.

Hereford, Amy. *Religious Life at the Crossroads: A School for Mystics and Prophets.* New York: Orbis Books, 2013.

Himes, Michael. "Returning to Our Ancestral Lands." *Review for Religious* 59, no. 1 (January–February 2000): 6–25.

Howell, Maribeth. "Discerning a Call to Religious Life." *Human Development* 36, no. 3 (Spring 2016): 48–53.

Jamison, Christopher. "Setting Themselves Apart." *The Tablet* 271, no. 9205 (June 17, 2017): 4–5.

John Paul II. *Vita Consecrata*. Vatican City: Libreria Editrice Vaticana, 1996. http://w2.vatican.va/content/john-paul-ii/en/apost_exhortations/documents/hf_jp-ii_exh_25031996_vita-consecrata.html.

Johnson, Mary, Patricia Wittberg, and Mary L. Gautier. *New Generations of Catholic Sisters: The Challenge of Diversity*. New York: Oxford University, 2014.

Kovats, Alexandra. "Re-Visioning the Vows Holistically." *LCWR Occasional Papers* (Summer 2003): 23–30.

Lee, Bernard. *The Beating of Great Wings: A Worldly Spirituality for Active, Apostolic Communities*. Mystic, CT: Twenty-Third Publications, 2004.

Leonard, Ellen M. "Contemporary Theologies of the Vows." *Review for Religious* 61, no. 5 (September–October 2002): 511–21.

MacCurtain, Margaret. "Religious Life: The Future of Our Past." *Doctrine and Life* 67, no. 9 (November 2017): 53–61.

Mascarenhas, Fio. "Consecrated Life: Putting on the Character of Jesus." *Vidyajyoti Journal of Theological Reflection* 79, no. 6 (June 2015): 447–51.

McNamara, JoAnn Kay. *Sisters in Arms: Catholic Nuns through Two Millennia*. Cambridge, MA: Harvard University Press, 2010.

Mousseau, Juliet, and Sarah Kohles, eds. *In Our Own Words: Religious Life in a Changing World*. Collegeville, MN: Liturgical Press, 2018.

Murray, Donal. "Glorious and Unfinished: The Year of Consecrated Life." *The Furrow* 66, no. 6 (June 2015): 311–19.

Nogosek, Robert J. "Religious Life as an Acceptable Sacrifice." *Review for Religious* 69, no. 3 (2010): 281–96.

Nolan, Albert. "Religious Life as a Prophetic Witness." *Grace & Truth* 31, no. 2 (August 2014): 6–16.

O'Donnell, Gabriel. "The Renewal of Religious Life: Strengthening the Trinitarian 'Communio' in the Church." In *Called to Holi-*

ness and Community: Vatican II on the Church. Scranton, PA: University of Scranton Press, 2009.

O'Murchu, Diarmuid. *Consecrated Religious Life: The Changing Paradigms.* Maryknoll, NY: Orbis Books, 2005.

O'Murchu, Diarmuid. *Religious Life in the 21st Century: The Prospect of Refounding.* Maryknoll, NY: Orbis Books, 2016.

Park, Jung Eun Sophia. *Conversations at the Well: Emerging Religious Life in the 21st-Century Global World: Collaboration, Networking, and Intercultural Living.* Eugene, OR: Wipf & Stock, 2019.

Paul, Ann Marie. "Gleanings from My First Ten Years." *Review for Religious* 69, no. 1 (2010): 63–70.

Pellegrino, Mary, "Life on the Margins: Charismatic Principles for Modern Religious," *America Magazine*, October 16, 2013. http://www.americamagazine.org/issue/life-margins.

Pitts, Mary Dominic. "The Threefold Response of the Vows." In *The Foundations of Religious Life,* 84–111. Notre Dame, IN: Ave Maria Press, 2009.

Radcliffe, Timothy. "Community Life and Mission: Toward a Future Full of Hope." Presentation at Catholic Theological Union, Chicago, IL, February 6, 2016. http://www.ctuconsecratedlife .org/videos/.

Radcliffe, Timothy. "Letter to Our Brothers and Sisters in Initial Formation." Feast of Blessed Jordan of Saxony 1999. http:// www.op.org/sites/www.op.org/files/public/documents/fichier /radcliffe1999_letterformation_en.pdf.

Radcliffe, Timothy. "Same God, Different Ways to Love." *Horizon* 39, no. 4 (Fall 2014): 9–13.

Renić, Dalibor. "Intergenerational Dialogue in Religious Life: The Importance of *Cura Personalis.*" *Doctrine and Life* 67, no. 2 (February 2017): 33–43.

Reynolds, Robyn. "Bound to Be Free!: Vowed Religious Life." *The Furrow* 68, no. 5 (May 2017): 279–86.

Riebe-Estrella, Gary. "The Vow to Obedience." *LCWR Occasional Papers,* Winter 2013: 16–18.

Robert, Sylvie. "To Live Here Below from the Beyond: Religious Vows and Apostolic Life." *Review for Religious* 70, no. 3 (2011): 234–46.

Sacred Congregation for Religious and for Secular Institutes. "Essential Elements in the Church's Teaching on Religious Life as Applied to Institutes Dedicated to Works of the Apostolate." Vatican City: Libreria Editrice Vaticana, 1983. http://www.vatican.va/roman_curia/congregations/ccscrlife/documents/rc_con_ccscrlife_doc_31051983_magisterium-on-religious-life_en.html.

Salker, David. "Christian Discipleship and Consecrated Life." *The Australasian Catholic Record* 92, no. 2 (April 2015): 131–40.

Sammon, Sean D. "The Domestication of US Religious Life." *Human Development* 23, no. 2 (Summer 2007): 33–38.

Sammon, Sean D. "Religious Life: Diminished, But Surely Not Dying." *Human Development* 34, no. 3 (Fall 2013): 14–17.

Sammon, Sean D. *Religious Life in America*. New York: Alba House, 2002.

Sammon, Sean D. "Religious Life Reimagined: Looking for Opportunity in a Misunderstood Vocation Crisis." *America* 213, no. 6 (September 14, 2015): 26–29.

Schneiders, Sandra. *Buying the Field: Religious Life in Mission to the World*. New York: Paulist Press, 2013.

Schneiders, Sandra. *Finding the Treasure: Locating Catholic Religious Life in a New Ecclesial and Cultural Context*. New York: Paulist Press, 2000.

Schneiders, Sandra. *Selling All: Commitment, Consecrated Celibacy, and Community in Catholic Religious Life*. New York: Paulist Press, 2001.

Schreck, Nancy. "'In the Footsteps of Our Lord Jesus Christ': Obedience and Church Authority in the Evangelical Tradition." *LCWR Occasional Papers,* Summer 2002: 13–18.

Schreiter, Robert. "Reimagining Consecrated Life in a Changing World." *New Theology Review* 28, no. 1 (September 2015): 33–38.

Senior, Donald. "Living in the Meantime: Biblical Foundations for Religious Life." In *Living in the Meantime: Concerning the Transformation of Religious Life*, edited by Paul J. Philibert, 55–71. Mahwah, NJ: Paulist, 1994.

Siegfried, Regina. "Religious Formation Conference: 'Education for Deepening Relationships: theological/communal/societal/

cultural/ecological.' " *American Catholic Studies* 120, no. 1 (2009): 55–71.

Simmonds, Gemma, ed. *A Future Full of Hope?* Collegeville, MN: Liturgical Press, 2012.

Spadaro, Antonio. "A Big Heart Open to God: An Interview with Pope Francis." *America,* September 30, 2013. https://www.americamagazine.org/faith/2013/09/30/big-heart-open-god-interview-pope-francis.

Spadaro, Antonio. " 'Wake Up the World!' Conversation with Pope Francis about the Religious Life." Translated by Donald Maldari. *La Civiltà Cattolica* I.3–17 (2014).

Steindl-Rast, David. *Gratefulness, the Heart of Prayer: An Approach to Life in Fullness.* New York: Paulist Press, 1984.

Studzinski, Raymond. "Intergenerational Living: Challenges and Strategies for Monastic Communities." *The American Benedictine Review* 68, no. 2 (June 2017): 136–53.

Teresa of Calcutta, *Come Be My Light: The Private Writings of the Saint of Calcutta.* Edited by Brian Kolodiejchuk. New York: Crown Publishing, 2007.

Thompson, Margaret Susan. "Charism or Deep Story? Towards Understanding Better the 19th-Century Origins of American Women's Congregations." *Review for Religious* 58, no. 3 (May–June 1999): 230–50.

United States Conference of Catholic Bishops. *Forming Consciences for Faithful Citizenship: A Call to Political Responsibility from the Catholic Bishops of the United States.* February 2020. https://www.usccb.org/issues-and-action/faithful-citizenship/upload/forming-consciences-for-faithful-citizenship.pdf.

Vidrine, Andrea. "Who Knows?: On Nondualism and Spiritual Direction." *Presence: An International Journal of Spiritual Direction* 21, no. 3 (September 2013): 43–49.

Wayte, Simon R. "The Risen Christ: Present and Embodied in Consecrated Life Today." *God Has Begun a Great Work in Us: Embodied Love in Consecrated Life and Ecclesial Movements.* Maryknoll, NY: Orbis, 2015.

Wiesner, Theodore. "Experiencing God in the Poor." *Spiritual Life* 33 (Winter 1987): 213–21.

Xavier, Joseph. "Call of Evangelical Counsels." *Vidyajyoti Journal of Theological Reflection* 79, no. 4 (April 2015): 245–58.

Zinn, Carol. "Crossing the Threshold: Weaving Global Solidarity for the Life of the World." Presentation, Plenary Assembly of International Union Superiors, Rome, May 9–13, 2016. http://www.internationalunionsuperiorsgeneral.org/wp-content/uploads/2016/04/Pl-2016_-Carol-Zinn_ENG.pdf, 11–12.